P9-ASC-326

ORIENTAL RUGS

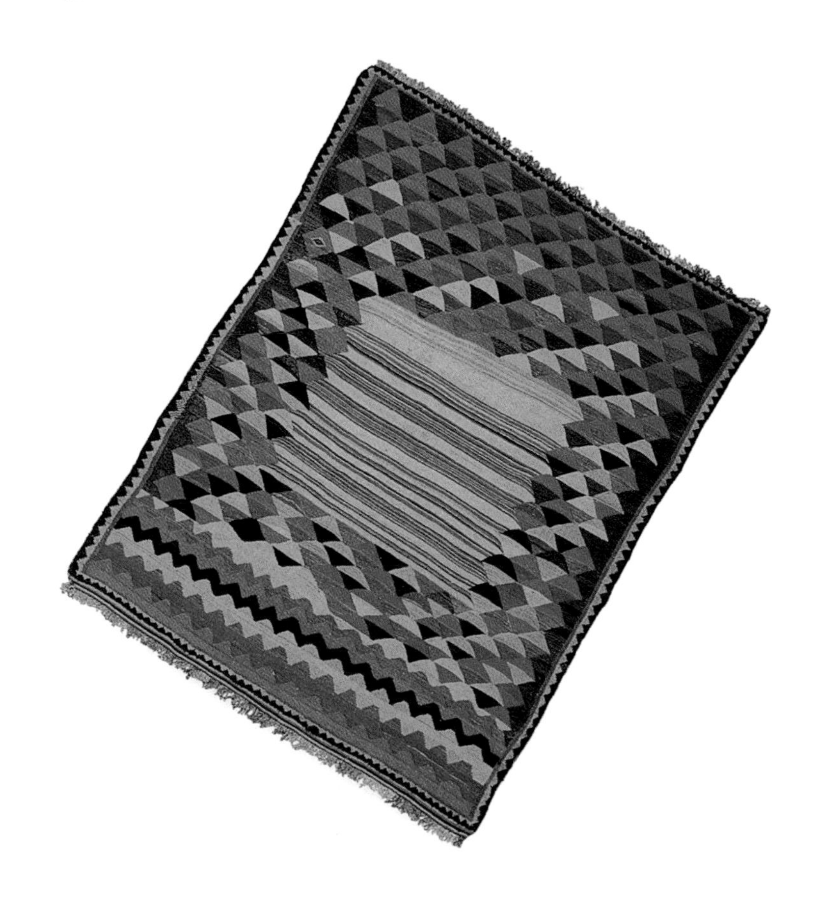

ORIENTAL RUGS

A Quantum Book

Published by Grange Books
an imprint of Grange Books Plc
The Grange
Kingsnorth Industrial Estate
Hoo, nr Rochester
Kent ME3 9ND

ISBN 1-84013-290-6

This book is produced by
Quantum Books Ltd
6 Blundell Street
London N7 9BH

Project Manager: Rebecca Kingsley
Art Director: Siân Keogh
Project Editor: Jo Wells
Designer: Martin Laurie
Assistant Designer: Sandra Marques
Editor: Lyn Coutts

The material in this publication previously appeared in *Oriental Rugs*, *Oriental Carpet Identifier*

QUMCCRC
Set in Gill Sans
Reproduced in Singapore by Eray Scan Pte Ltd
Printed in Singapore by Star Standard Industries (Pte) Ltd

CONTENTS

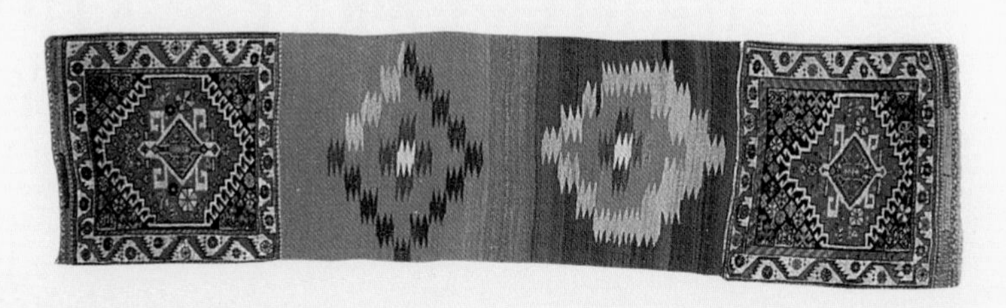

INTRODUCTION

MAGIC CARPET RIDE THROUGH HISTORY

BELOW Bijar rug with all-over design of floral and plant motifs defined by red and yellow arabesques.

This book is a general introduction to Oriental rugs for those who might wish to collect them. To appreciate Oriental rugs it is necessary to know something of the characteristics of weave and design, the lifestyle of the rug weavers and how the rugs of one country differ from those of another. As so many designs and patterns have been created, it is preferable that the structure of rugs is also used as a method of identification.

It is not known when the weaving of rugs began. The oldest carpet in existence is the Pazyryk carpet that was found frozen in a burial tomb in Inner Asia and is dated to the fourth century BC. Its design, dyes and weave are of the highest quality, indicating that the weaver was knowledgeable. From this and other data, it is assumed that rug-weaving had evolved by the second millennium BC. Records and evidence of carpet weaving from the Pazyryk to the fourteenth century are fragmentary. Some rug remnants from the third, sixth and eleventh centuries survive, but without any connection or continuity. A continuous connection for rugs from Anatolia exists from the fourteenth century and for Persia from the sixteenth century. Thus the study of Oriental rugs covers only the last five hundred years with any great degree of certainty.

Oriental carpets have been used and collected in the West for centuries. Our knowledge of them is based primarily on their depiction in paintings from the fifteenth century onwards. The presence of rugs in paintings is one of the principal ways of dating the few carpets remaining from before the nineteenth century. In them it is possible to study the evolution of various designs and place the rugs into periods and groups.

Their earliest appearance is in religious paintings where rugs appear under a throne on which the Virgin Mary is seated. A century later, rugs appeared as signs of wealth and power in court paintings. The types of rugs that were depicted in these paintings have acquired the names of the painters, such as Holbein, Memling, Crivelli and Lotto.

Prior to the seventeenth century almost all of these rugs are from the area we know today as Turkey. However, during that century rugs from Persia begin to appear because the European states were trading with the Safavid Empire and many goods were reaching Europe via the Silk Road. Although there were ups and downs in this trade, Persia remained one of the principal sources of Oriental carpets from then on.

The Oriental rug languished as a luxury and decorative item from the mid-1700s until the mid-1800s. With the expansion of the middle class in Europe and America by the mid-1800s, however, there was a rebirth of interest in collecting Oriental rugs. This led to a revival of rug weaving in Turkey, the Caucasus, Persia, Central Asia, India and China.

Most of the rugs that are prized by collectors today were woven after this time. These are the rugs on which this book is focused. The various types that have been collected, are being collected and may be collected in the future are described.

BELOW This map will prove useful when you look at the geographical classification of rugs and carpets.

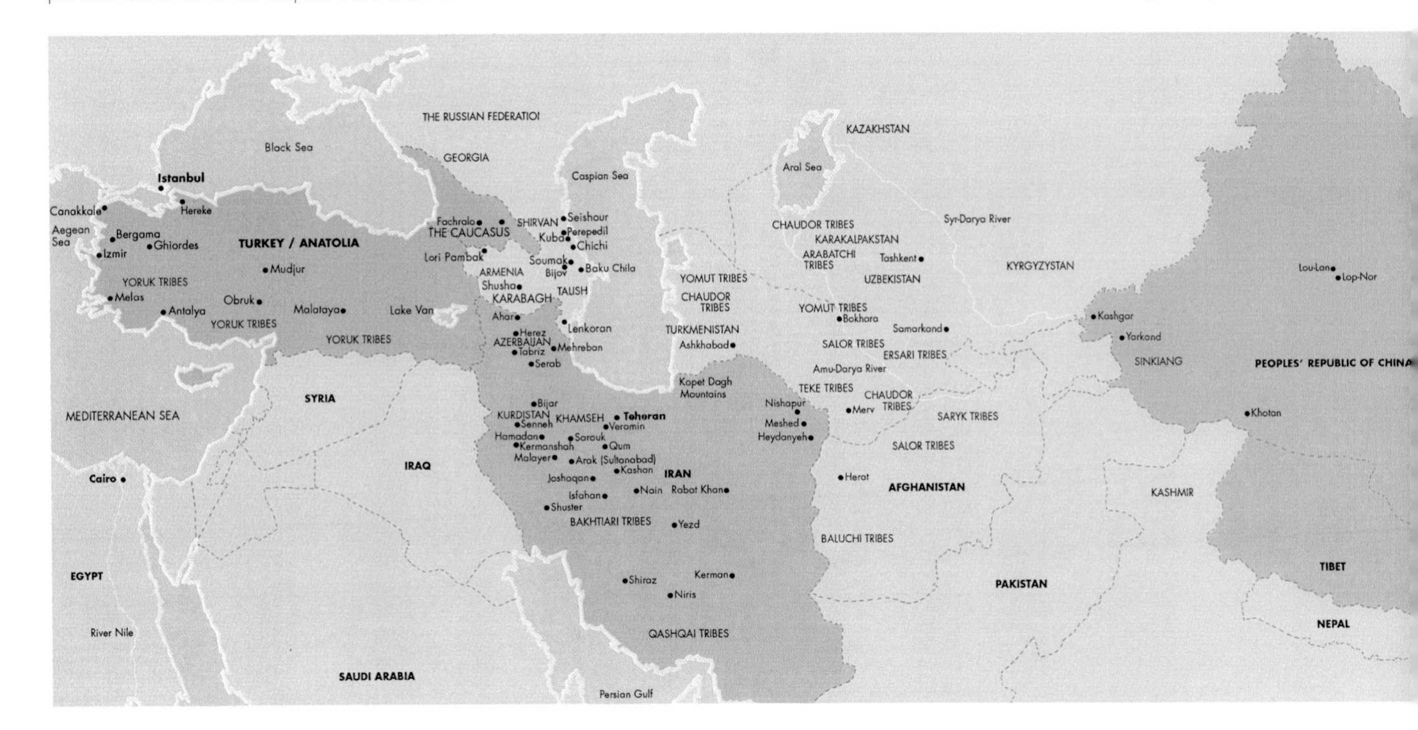

How rugs are made

Knowledge of the factors that go into the making of a rug helps in identification. An Oriental rug must be hand-made, but they are made of different materials, on different looms, with many dyes, in an array of patterns and designs by weavers living divergent lifestyles.

Rugs are made of essentially three types of thread: the warp, weft and pile.

Warp is wrapped on the loom and is the foundation thread of a rug. It is usually exposed as the fringe. Warps at the side of a rug are finished in special ways to create an edge.

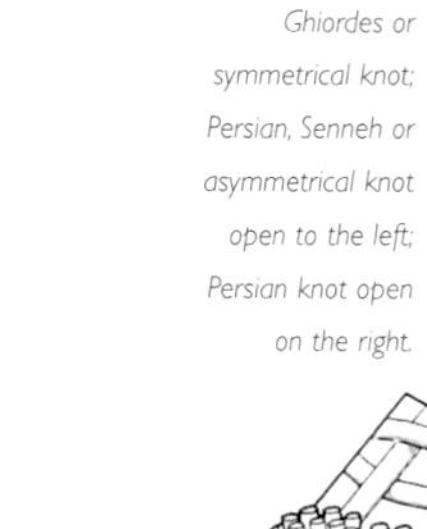

BELOW Types of knot (from left to right): Turkish, Ghiordes or symmetrical knot; Persian, Senneh or asymmetrical knot open to the left; Persian knot open on the right.

Weft is inserted sinuously across the width of the loom, perpendicular or at right angles to the warp, and after each a row of knots holds them in place. The weft binds all the threads into a cohesive structure.

Pile (knot) creates the pattern. There are two types of pile knot, symmetric and asymmetric. Older names for the symmetric knot are Turkish, Ghiordes and double; and for the asymmetric: Persian, Senneh and single. The asymmetric knot may be tied to open right or open left. Each type of knot can also be woven to give the pile an inclination to the right or left.

The warp depression is the way in which the warps can be made to lie parallel to one another or on different levels. It is done by manipulating the wefts. Warp depression increases knot density.

Knot density is the number of knots in a specific square unit of measurement (usually square centimetres or inches) as counted by looking at the back of the rug. Horizontally, the two nodes at the base of the knot are counted as one knot. Vertically, one node between each row of wefts represents a knot. This counting method does not apply to rugs with warp depression.

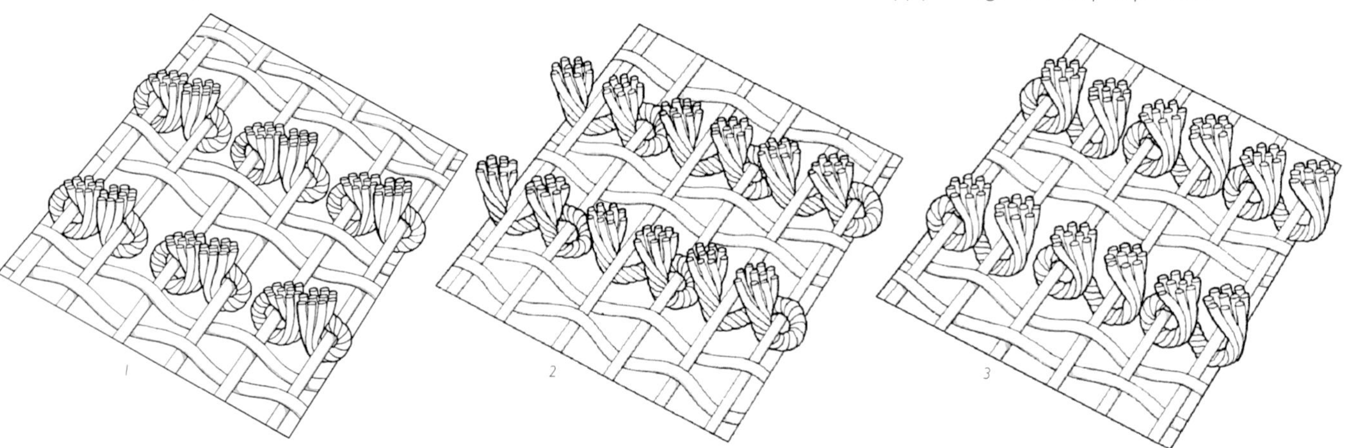

LEFT This circa 1800 Bijar carpet, with unreconciled bottom borders, shows Persianate patterns. The main field has herati patterns, the border arabesques.

Knot density is a reflection of many aspects of a rug's construction, such as size of the warp, weft and pile threads, how tightly the weaver tamps each row of knots and the presence or absence of warp depression. Knot density is not the determinant of quality. Most rugs of a type fall within a certain knot density. A type of rug noted for high knot density is not better than one with medium knot density; it is probably more expensive, but not better. Cost, not aesthetic merit, wool quality or rarity, is most closely correlated with knot density.

Materials

Rug weavers use many types of fibre, and their choice of fibre or fibres can indicate the weaver's lifestyle – nomadic or settled. The most commonly used fibres are wool and cotton. Silk, camel hair, goat hair and horse hair are uncommon.

Wool is the most common fibre and is used for the warp, weft and pile. Its natural colours – white, grey, tan, dark brown and black – are used, but it is also dyed to create patterns. Different types of wool vary in lustre, durability and feel.

Cotton is the next most common fibre and is mainly used for the warp and weft. It is infrequently found in the pile, but when so used is an important identification factor. Cotton is white unless dyed.

Silk is the most expensive fibre and may be used for warp, weft and pile. Because it can be spun more finely than wool or cotton, it is often found in the most finely-knotted and the most opulent rugs, when it is used to show wealth and status. It is used in its natural off-white colour or dyed.

Camel hair is used mostly as a pile thread in its natural colour, which may vary from pale tan to brown.

Goat hair and horse hair are used mostly for the edges of rugs because they are durable. The natural fibres are dark brown or black.

Types of loom

BELOW All bar the indigo are early synthetic dyes on this Perepedil Kuba rug (circa 1800).

A horizontal loom is constructed parallel to the ground, it is portable even with unfinished weaving on it. It consists of two beams around which the warp threads are wrapped. It is raised slightly off the ground, and the weaver sits on top of the warp threads. Rugs woven on horizontal looms commonly do not have perfectly equal sides and ends.

A vertical loom is constructed vertical to the ground, it may be free-standing and leaned against a wall, or it may be built permanently in place. It is not readily portable. The weaver sits in front of the loom. Rugs woven on vertical looms have relatively even sides and ends.

Dyes in rugs

Prior to the discovery of the first synthetic dye in 1856, the dyes in Oriental rugs came from natural sources – plants (including flowers, leaves, stems and roots), minerals and insects.

Red Madder was the most common plant source for a warm red that has yellow components in its make-up. Cochineal, derived from scale insects, is a cool red because of the presence of blue components. Other red dyes were derived from safflower and brazilwood.

Yellow From diverse plant sources including saffron crocus stamens, pomegranate rind, dyer's weed, larkspur, camomile, salvia and certain sumachs.

Blue Indigo was the source for all shades of blue.

Brown The husks of the fruit of walnut and oak trees provided shades of browns. Most browns, because of their tannic acid content, are corrosive and cause the fibres to become brittle. This is not a negative feature because it results in an etched effect.

Green This colour resulted from combining indigo with a yellow dye. Many naturally-produced greens are a blue-green, though a blue-green hue can be due to the yellow component of the dye fading. True greens are scarce, but do exist.

Orange Resulted primarily from combining red and yellow dyes, or by using a weakened madder dye bath.

Violet/purple Made by combining red and indigo dyes, or by the special treatment of madder.

Black Produced from a combination of a tannic dye, such as oak acorn husks or pomegranate tree galls, with iron salts. Black dye is very corrosive.

Synthetic dyes

In the 1860s Oriental rug weavers were utilizing synthetic dyes, but by 1900 synthetic dyes had almost displaced natural ones. Accidentally discovered by William

H. Perkin, a chemistry student, the first synthetics were produced from coal tar and were called aniline dyes. The Germans developed azo dyes. By the 1860s, synthetic dyes in reds, oranges, yellows and greens were available; indigo was not available until 1897.

Rug literature contains many references to the deleterious effects of synthetic dyes, the most common being fading and bleeding. Some of the reds were notorious for bleeding, and magentas, pinks and greens faded.

At the beginning of the 1900s a new group of chrome synthetic dyes came into being. These dyes did not have the problems of bleeding and fading. After the First World War, chrome dyes were used in Oriental rug weaving along with aniline and azo dyes, though it was not until the 1950s that they dominated the industry.

Mordants

For most dyes to adhere or fix themselves to wool fibre, the wool must be treated with a metallic salt, called a mordant. The mordant may be iron, aluminium, copper or tin. The type and strength of the mordant will affect the colour tone of the carpet. Indigo and the brown dyes are called direct dyes, which means that they do not require a mordant.

LEFT This Sarouk mat (circa 1930) was chemically treated and repainted a deeper blue-red colour to suit the tastes of the American market.

Spotting the difference

One of the visual differences between rugs coloured with natural and synthetic dyes is the way each dye penetrates the fibres. Natural dyes show subtle colour gradations within the thread; synthetic dyes penetrate the thread evenly.

With exposure to light and use, synthetic dyes fade and change colour (magenta, for example, becomes grey); natural dyes mellow but there is no colour change. Chrome dyes do not fade, and new natural-dyed rugs can have the same harsh look of new synthetic-dyed ones. To confirm the degree of fading, fold the rug to reveal the base of a knot. If a natural dye was used, the colour will be essentially uniform from knot tip to base. If it is a fading synthetic dye, the tip and more will be a different colour from the knot base. Unfortunately, there are many exceptions to this rule.

BELOW An obvious abrash is shown in the blue field of this Chahar Mahal carpet (circa 1890).

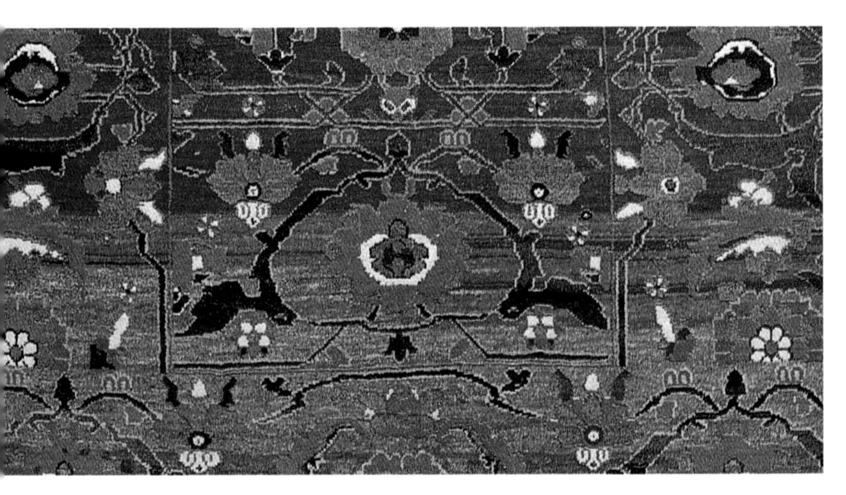

Abrash

A nomadic or village weaver will weave only one rug at a time, therefore only a few skeins of wool will be dyed in each colour. With this method – called small-batch dyeing – when skeins of a given colour are dyed, the colours will not match perfectly, resulting in abrash. In commercial weaving, dyers calculate the wool needed and dye that requirement in one go, resulting in a consistent colour.

Abrash is a positive feature and it refers to a subtle change of tone in a colour that results when the weaver changes from one skein to the next. It is one of the 'imperfections' that hand-made rugs are 'supposed' to have. Abrash is sometimes deliberately manipulated.

Stripping

From the end of the 1800s, a chemical treatment called stripping was used to alter one or more of the dyes in the rug. The rug may be sold in this new stripped colour, or the stripped colours may be repainted.

In the 1920s and 1930s rust-red rugs from Sarouk in Persia were stripped and repainted a magenta-red in order to appeal to the American market.

It is still common practice to give new rugs, even natural-dyed ones, a light chemical wash in order to soften the colours. Most collectors avoid rugs that have received this treatment.

Types and sizes

For the collector, the size and function of a weaving is as important as other features, as both these factors help determine if a rug is commercial (made intentionally for sale) or collectable. Collectable implies that it was primarily made to be used by the weaver to satisfy a need of her lifestyle, not to satisfy a foreign buyer.

Carpets Usually larger than 275cm by 180cm (9ft × 6ft) in size, and purchased for decorative purposes.
Rugs Usually smaller than 275cm by 180cm (9ft × 6ft), and popular for collecting.
Runners Usually 90–120cm (3–4ft) wide and about 250–600cm (8–20ft) in length, they are treated as commercial in view of their specific use.
Prayer rugs Ranging from 60–120cm (2–4ft) in width or 120–245cm (4–8ft) in length, they are very popular with collectors. Prayer rugs are known by these names: sejadeh, namazlyk, jol namaz. and saph.
Donkeybags These utilitarian weavings for carrying goods were, at maximum, 60cm by 150cm (2ft x 5ft) in size. Popular among collectors, many older donkeybags were cut and sold as small rugs, known as bagfaces (in Persian, khorjin).
Juvals Single, rectangular bags in many sizes. Juvals were typically made in pairs, and because of their popularity they were cut and sold as small rugs.

Other utilitarian weavings made for specific daily and festive needs include tent bands, animal trappings for wedding ceremonies, and coverings for animals such as horses and camels. These weavings are among some of the most desired by collectors.

CLOCKWISE FROM LEFT Rug types and sizes: carpet, rug, prayer rug, runner, juval and donkeybag.

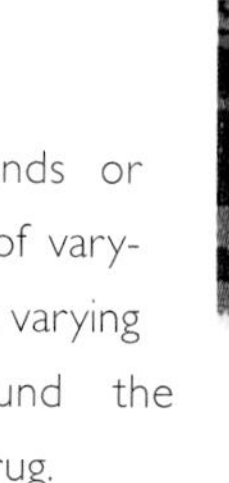

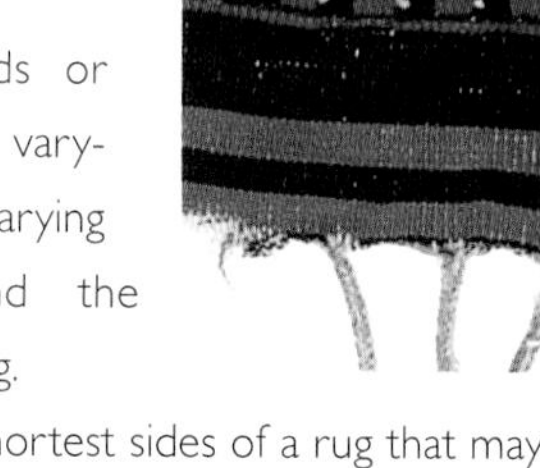

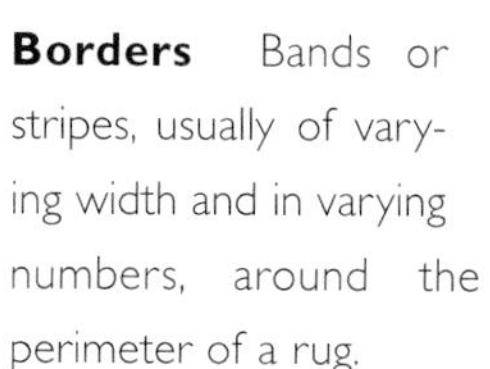

Design and pattern

TOP RIGHT The red, white and blue star, mihrab and leaf forms of this Bergama prayer rug (circa 1900) is typical of a weaving from west Anatolia.

Special terms are used to describe the format of a weaving, whether pile or flatweave, donkeybag or juval.

Field The large area in the centre of a rug that contains the main design. It is surrounded by the borders.

Field or ground colour The colour or colours on which the design is arranged.

Pattern Specific elements used to create a design on the field and borders.

Design The overall impression created on the field. An all-over design is one in which the same pattern is used repetitively. A centred or medallion design is typically one with a medallion around which secondary patterns are arranged.

Spandrels Centred designs often have quarter-medallions or distinctively different patterns in the corners of the field, these patterns are known as spandrels.

This kelim – a kurdish juval (circa 1900) – from east Anatolia was originally a bag.

Borders Bands or stripes, usually of varying width and in varying numbers, around the perimeter of a rug.

Ends The two shortest sides of a rug that may consist of a flatwoven area, 2.5–30cm (1–12in) deep. In older, used rugs this will show wear and may be missing.

Fringe Extends from the ends and is the exposed warps. It may be 2.5–25cm (1–10in) long when new. The fringe may be braided or knotted.

Edge The two long sides of a rug that may be finished with an overcast or selvedge for durability. An overcast is a group of warps wrapped with a separate thread in a circular fashion; this type of finish has a rounded look. A selvedge has pairs of warps covered by a figure-of-eight wrapping, which creates a flatter and wider edge than overcasting.

Skirt Weavings such as juvals and donkeybags have an additional wide border, known as a skirt, running along on one side of the rug.

Patterns used in rugs may vary in shape, size or drawing, but the basic form remains recognizable. Patterns vary from country to country according to the type of weaver – that is, nomadic, village or city.

Patterns may have straight or stepped outlines (abstract or geometric), curved or rounded outlines (representational or curvilinear), or herati, mina khani, boteh and arabesque patterns most closely associated with rugs from Iran (Persianate).

ABOVE Arabesque, tendril or vine is a straight or curved line connecting pattern elements.

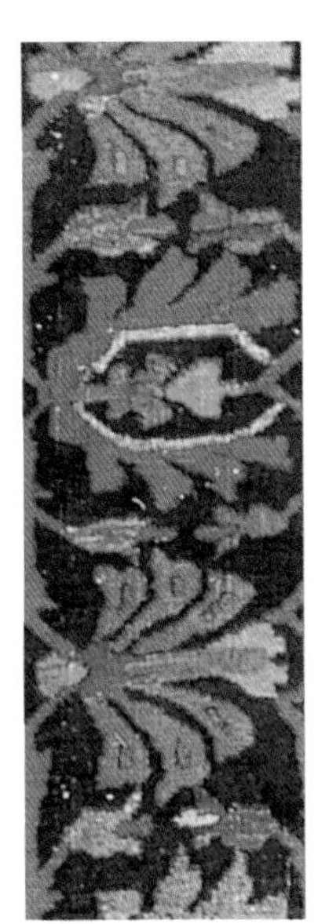

ABOVE Palmette is a vertical cross-section of a flower.

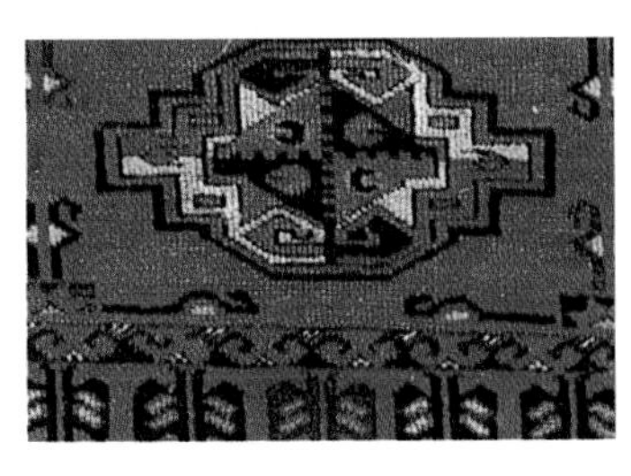

ABOVE Gul, a polygon with various motifs within it.

ABOVE Trefoil is a three-part pattern that acts as the focus for the design.

ABOVE Rosette is a horizontal cross-section of a flower.

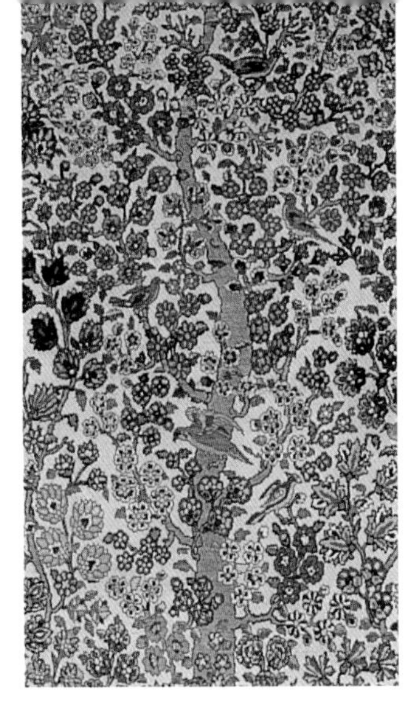

ABOVE Tree of Life frequently used on prayer rugs.

ABOVE Leaf is a flat pattern with a leaf shape.

ABOVE Boteh (paisley, pine cone or shawl) is similar to a leaf but wider and rounder at the bottom.

ABOVE Mina khani is a complex arrangement of rosettes and palmettes on a vine.

ABOVE Mihrab is an arch-shaped form used on prayer rugs.

ABOVE Medallion is a larger central field pattern, often the focus.

Pattern elements and meaning

The elements of a pattern are embellishments used to enhance complexity or importance. Some of the more common ones are listed below.

Latchhook Hooked device used around the edge of geometric forms.
Lattice Series of connected lines that create an openwork structure.
Filler elements Geometric, floral and animal forms used to fill spaces between pattern elements.

The meaning of patterns is one of the most written-about aspects of Oriental rugs and one of the least understood. Scholars have traced the evolution of designs, their origins and how they have changed over time, under different rulers and empires.

There are various and numerous (to the point of exhaustive) theories as to the original meanings of some patterns. Most weavers today, however, frequently attach quite different meanings to patterns from those suggested by scholars.

ABOVE Filler elements of animal and plant forms along with geometrical motifs.

TOP RIGHT The clearly obvious hooked device of a latchhook element.

RIGHT Lattice encasing simplified floral motifs.

CHAPTER ONE

CLASSIFICATION BY LIFESTYLE AND GEOGRAPHY

Rugs are divided in two principal ways: according to the lifestyle of the weavers and the geographic area in which the rugs were made. Lifestyle refers to how the weavers make a living, where they live and the end-purpose of the weavings. Each rug displays characteristics of the weaver's lifestyle – nomadic, village or city.

Nomadic

The nomadic lifestyle in its purest form implies people who live in portable dwellings and move from place to place with some frequency. They tend sheep, horses, camels or goats and are totally dependent on their animals and the land.

Nomadic peoples weave on portable looms and use dyes from free-growing plants. Nomadic weavers use a relatively limited pattern and design range. The following characteristics are typical of these rugs.

Materials Wool warps and wefts; silk used spaingly.
Colours From three to seven.
Edge and end finish The edge will usually be finished with a selvedge; edges will be irregular and the ends may differ in width. Plain or patterned kelim 2.5–38cm (1–15in) in width. Fringe, often braided, 12.5–25cm (5–10in) in length.
Pile height Medium to long.
Types of pattern All-over, simple and angular geometric, floral and animate forms predominate. Borders are unreconciled.
Sizes and shapes Numerous.
Technical features Woven with warps on one level, not depressed, with knot density about 80 per 6.5 centimetres square (1 inch square).

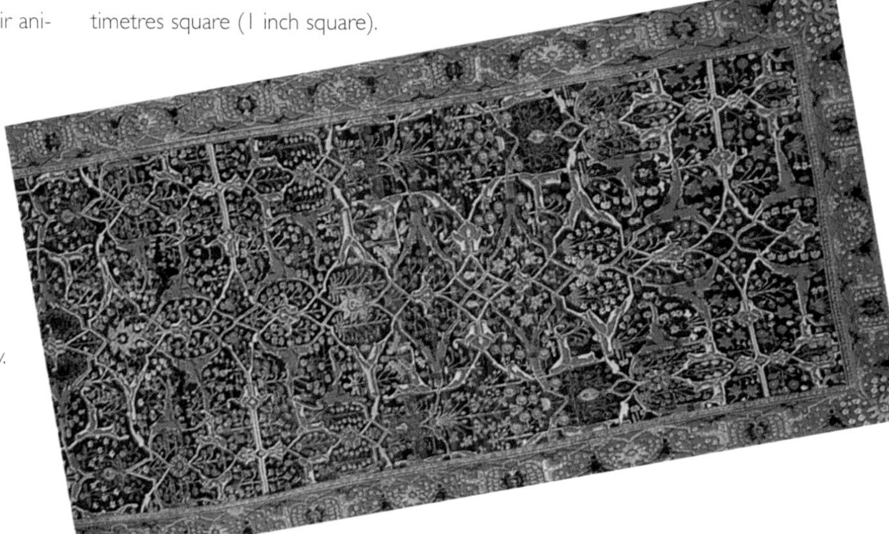

BELOW Strapwork and arabesque design Bijar carpet (circa 1840), is a version of a garden carpet design dating from the 1600s. Reconciled corners identify it as a workshop carpet.

Village

Weavers live in agricultural communities and may keep sheep, horses and goats, but will also grow crops including cotton, which may be used in place of wool. Settled lifestyle means upright, permanent looms. They may have a wider range of dye materials than nomads. Able to weave for longer periods, articles are produced for sale and for personal use. Because of a larger social community, patterns and designs are diverse. The following characteristics are typical of rugs woven by village people.

BELOW Shahsavan bagface (circa 1850) where a latchhook motif fills the border and field. The light-coloured areas on four of the animals are silk highlights.

Materials Cotton warps; cotton or wool wefts. Silk used in small quantities or in special pieces.

Colours From five to ten, with a variety of blues and distinct greens.

Edge and end finish Overcast edges even more common, with only minimal width difference at the ends. The kelim is 2.5–5cm (1–2in) wide. The fringe (often warp loops) is 2.5–10cm (1–4in) in length.

Pile height Medium to short.

Types of pattern All-over or centred, geometric and floral, but angular not rounded. Corners are unreconciled.

Sizes and shapes Floor rugs from 60cm by 120cm (2ft x 4ft) to 300cm by 550cm (10ft x 18ft). Village weavers also make utilitarian items.

Technical features Warps on one level, but many have depressed warps. The knot density is mostly 60–120 knots per 6.5 centimetres square (1 inch square).

City

City dwellers weave the most intricate carpets. Weaving is an established commercial activity and is conducted in ateliers where looms are permanent. Weaving is divided among a variety of skilled craftspeople. No one person can be said to have 'woven' a city carpet. The following characteristics are typical of city rugs.

Materials Warps and wefts primarily cotton, and pile is usually wool. Silk may be used for warp, weft and pile.

Colours From eight to twenty.

Edge and end finish Edges are primarily finished with an overcast of cotton. Because of the permanent look, the ends are of equal width. The kelim of various widths and the fringe is 2.5–10cm (1–4in) long.

Pile height Medium to short.

LEFT Village weaving depicting a water ewer – symbolizing cleanliness – inside a prayer arch on this Konya prayer rug.

Design and pattern Mostly curvilinear with reconciled corners. Most patterns have a medallion, arabesques and spandrels. All-over designs are also used.
Sizes and shapes Almost all are rugs and carpets.
Technical features Many rugs are woven with warp depression, and most have more than 100 knots per 6.5 centimetres square (1 inch square), though as many as 300–600 are common.

A geographic approach

The traditional rug-weaving areas are Turkey, the Caucasus, Iran, Central Asia and China. The rugs of each area have distinctive technical features, of which the most important are described.

Turkey

Knot type Symmetrical.
Knot density Coarse to medium; 40–90 knots per 6.5 centimetres square (1 inch square) though city rugs have a higher knot density.
Warp and weft fibres Wool warp (often dyed red) and weft in nomadic and most village rugs; cotton is used in city rugs. Silk used in minor details in nomadic and village rugs, while city rugs may be all silk.
Colours Wide range; purples, yellows, oranges, greens and salmons distinctive.
Sizes and shapes Diverse, but small rugs and prayer rugs common. Villagers and nomads produce bags.
Pattern and design Full range, though geometric and angular floral patterns predominate.
Technical features Edge finishes are mostly selvedge. Fringes either short or long, and kelims 10–18cm (4–7in) wide. Pile height varied. Warp depression occurs mostly in city rugs.

The Caucasus

Knot type Symmetrical.
Knot density Coarse to fine, usually 40–120 knots per 6.5 centimetres square (1 inch square).
Warp and weft fibres Wool warp and weft (wefts are natural and dyed) though cotton also used.
Colours Red, blue, yellow, green, orange, purple and corrosive brown.
Sizes and shapes Rugs are from 60cm by 120cm (2ft x 4ft) to 180cm by 245cm (6ft x 8ft). Large city rugs are two and a half times long as wide. Many donkeybags and prayer rugs made.

BELOW Three-medallion kazak (circa 1910) with random figures in the field indicates Caucasian origins.

RIGHT Border pattern of mountains and waves on this Chinese seat cover (circa 1880).

ABOVE Long, narrow Uzbeck mafrash (circa 1880) were made into bags.

Design and pattern Geometric and angular, with medallions and all-over designs are common. Small filler elements are scattered on the field. Border corners are unreconciled. City rugs have Persianate patterns.

Technical features Edge finishes are selvedge and overcast, and fringes (which are often braided) 8–18cm (3–7in). Kelim ends maximum 5–10cm (2–4in) wide. Pile height varies.

Iran or Persia

Knot type Symmetrical and asymmetrical.

Knot density Coarse to fine, with 30–1,000 knots or more per 6.5 centimetre square (1 inch square).

Warp and weft fibres Wool, cotton and silk.

Colours Full spectrum.

Sizes and shapes Diverse.

Design and pattern Diverse and varied.

Technical features All types of edge finishes, warp and weft fibres and fringes are found. Kelim ends may be 2.5–15cm (1–6in) wide. Pile length varies.

Central Asian and Turkoman

This area include Kazakhstan, Uzbekistan, Turkmenistan, Kyrgyzstan and Tajikistan.

Knot type Symmetrical and asymmetrical.

Knot density Coarse to fine, 30–200 knots per 6.5 centimetres square (1 inch square).

Warp and weft fibres Wool.

Colours Reds predominate.

Sizes and shapes Diverse.

Design and pattern Geometric and all-over designs with unreconciled borders.

Technical features Edge finishes are mostly selvedge, and kelim ends may be 5–38cm (2–15in) in width. Fringes are 15–25cm (6–10in) long. Pile depth varies.

China

Knot type Asymmetrical; looping method used in Tibet.

Knot density Medium to coarse, 40–80 knots per 6.5 centimetres square (1 inch square).

Warp and weft fibres Cotton predominates, but wool used for wefts in older Xinjiang and Tibetan rugs.

Dyes and colours Colours differ in each area.

Sizes and shapes Chinese rugs are usually large, Xinjiang medium, and Tibetan small.

Design and pattern Chinese centred and all-over designs. Border corners reconciled (bar Xinjiang rugs).

Technical features Edge finishes overcast in cotton; selvedges used in Xinjiang. Fringes 5–12.5cm (2–5in) long, and kelim ends 2.5–10cm (1–4in) wide. The pile depth is thick except in some Xinjiang rugs.

CHAPTER TWO

THE RUGS OF CHINA, EAST TURKESTAN AND TIBET

The rugs of these regions are considered together because the influence of the Chinese design tradition is evident in them all. However, each area has its own traditions of design, colour and weave.

Chinese rugs

Chinese rugs display patterns and colours found in Chinese textiles, wood carving and ceramics. The craft of rug weaving was probably brought into China with the invasions from Mongolia.

The Chinese used rugs primarily as floor and furniture coverings, though a special rug was woven to fit around columns in palaces and monasteries. Another type of weaving is the saddle cover. Chinese rugs were woven in workshops and are regarded as city rugs.

Primarily floral patterns are used in combination with the dragon, phoenix and other auspicious symbols represented by animals, fruits and flowers. A group of geometric patterns are used in both border and field. Designs are all-over and centred, and colours vary according to the period when they were woven, but the most common are blue, ivory and yellow; red is rarely used. Shades of corrosive brown were used in small pattern areas. The dominant colour in the oldest rugs (those of the early nineteenth century) was yellow; blue became dominant during the course of that century. At the turn of the twentieth century the clipping of pattern outlines began, and this is found in almost all Chinese rugs dating from the 1920s onward.

Areas of production

Ning Hsia produced rugs with yellow as a major colour; Paotou rugs were predominantly blue with ivory; and Peking rugs were room size with blue fields and ivory or gold borders.

Knot type Asymmetric.

Knot density The oldest pieces are the coarsest at about 40–70 knots per 6.5 centimetres square (1 inch square). Mid- and late-nineteenth-century rugs have 60–90 knots in the same area.

Warp and weft fibres Cotton, undyed, used for both.

Edge and end finish Selvedge was used on early pieces but cotton overcast on later pieces. Only about 2.5cm (1in) of kelim was woven and the fringe was not more than 12.5cm (5in).

Sizes and shapes Most are carpets though there are rugs; chair-seat and chair-back covers were produced in Paotou and Ning Hsia.

LEFT Typical Peking rug (circa 1880) in ivory and blue. The field motifs are everyday, recognizable items.

BELOW The light rust-red, mid-blue and yellow are distinctive colours of East Turkestan in this Khotan rug (circa 1900).

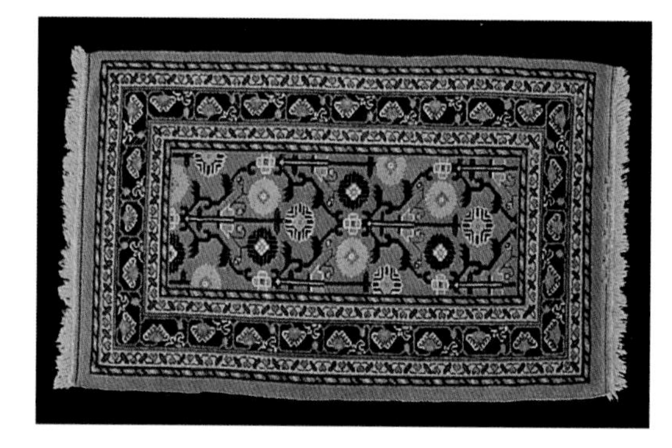

FAR EASTERN WEAVING

Mongolia and Turkestan

These two areas are usually considered together as a region (sometimes called East Turkestan) and the principal cities are Samarkand, Tashkent, Yarkand, Kashgar and Khotan, most of which were on the celebrated Silk Route. Influences on rug weaving were thus many and various, and confusion has resulted over the naming of pieces after their places of marketing not manufacture.

In spite of the confusion, it has come to be accepted by many that all silk pieces are ascribed to Khotan, as also are those pieces with a design of an all-over lattice and a trellis of stems and flower heads, often on a field of yellow or blue. Brilliant polychrome saphs were produced in Khotan late into the nineteenth century.

The pomegranate rugs – like some of the floral and most of the medallion rugs – usually have one of the three predominant East Turkestan borders. There are also examples of some highly formalized motifs that some describe as guls and others as medallions.

China

The weavers in the Land of Silk, although historically influenced by Mongolian design precepts, created pieces in very different styles and for different purposes from those of East Turkestan, All the same, some design motifs go back over one millennium: birds, shrubs growing from hillocks, clouds, pilgrims and flowers among arabesques of leaves and tendrils. The Mongolian influence is detectable in an occasionally more geometric style. Many of these motifs had symbolic meanings related phonetically; others were part of Chinese mythology. Yet others represented tenets such as the Four Symbols of Gentlemanly Accomplishments (music, chess, poetry and painting). A group of nineteenth century carpets portray Buddhist themes.

Tibet

Tibetan weaving is functional with pieces for sitting and/or sleeping upon, or for use as saddles or animal covers. Most pieces made as genuine carpets date from the last 100 years and incorporate foreign design motifs.

BELOW The dragon is a common theme for Chinese seat covers. This section (circa 1880) is shaped to match the scalloped contours of the chair back.

East Turkestan rugs

TOP RIGHT The Chinese cloud lattice creates two forms in the field: a cross and an eight-pointed star on this Khotan rug (circa 1840). The rosette border is unique to East Turkestan.

East Turkestan rugs are from Xinjiang, the western-most province of China. The native population is Turkic, not Han Chinese. Rugs have been woven here for centuries, mostly in workshops, and they differ in pattern and colour, which reflects the influence of Islamic, Buddhist and Chinese cultures and beliefs.

Patterns are floral and abstract, and a unique rosette in these rugs is called the coffered gul. Another pattern not found elsewhere is the vase/pomegranate pattern. Chinese frets and wave patterns are used.

RIGHT With edge patterns of mountains and waves, the exact use of this Khotan rug (circa 1800) is unknown. Eight clouds surround a fret medallion on a field of atypical red.

Both all-over and centred designs are used, with the three round medallions common. The medallions may have Chinese floral patterns or coffered guls. This type of design is Buddhist in origin. Some pieces have Persianate medallion and all-over patterns.

The colours are mainly pastel tones and yellow was used frequently. A strong green is found, and the browns are usually natural and not corrosive.

Areas of production

Rug weaving is assigned to Khotan, Yarkand and Kashgar based on design and structural features. The most prolific production is attributed to Khotan (all patterns) with silk rugs usually attributed to Yarkand and Kashgar. The principal features of the rugs are:

Knot type Asymmetric.

Knot density From 40 to 90 knots per 6.5 centimetres square (1 inch square). Silk rugs have a higher density.

Warp and weft fibres Warps are cotton, wefts may be cotton and wool. Most have three passes of the weft between each row of knots.

Edge and endfinish Overcast, but selvedges occur. The kelim is usually 2.5–5cm (1–2in).

Sizes and shapes Wide runners whose length is two to two-and-a-half times their width, room-size carpets and a few prayer rugs. A few utilitarian pieces were woven, most being saddle covers and donkeybags.

Tibetan rugs

Tibetan rugs have strong colours and patterns relating to Buddhism or bearing Chinese influences.

They are essentially village weavings with a unique technique. They are woven by a looping technique in which the pile threads are looped over a thin rod. When a row is finished, the loops are cut. The resulting knots may be asymmetric, symmetric or other versions of knots. Most Tibetan rugs are made for sitting, sleeping and praying upon, though some utilitarian pieces, like saddle bags, are also produced.

LEFT Khotan rug (circa 1910) showing a circular medallion (Buddhist), coffered guls (East Turkestan) and in the corners a shou design (Chinese).

LEFT Tibetan saddle cover (circa 1910) in a butterfly shape and decorated with snow lions.

Patterns are floral, representational (including motifs like dragons, phoenix, snow lions, tigers and bats), abstract and geometric. Designs are all-over or centred and borders often appear only on the ends. Tibetan rugs are bright (red dominates) with synthetic dyes. Orange, blue and yellow are often used as ground colours.

TOP RIGHT Notched-corner shaped Tibetan saddle cover with red felt edging typical of Tibetan rugs. The patterns are derived from Chinese weaving.

Areas of production

The cities of Shigatse and Gyantse are the largest centres, but rug weaving is practised widely.

Knot type Cut-loop knot (as described above).

Knot density From 30 to 100 knots per 6.5 centimetres square(1 inch square).

Warp and weft Wool warps, and cotton or wool wefts.

Edge and end finishes Many do not have typical edge finishes of selvedge and overcast, but are simply edge warps and wefts because felt edges and backing were added. The kelim is about 2.5cm (1in).

Sizes and shapes Sleeping rug (khaden) 90cm by 180cm (3ft × 6ft); sitting mat (khagangma) 90cm by 90cm (3ft x 3 ft); door-way rug (goyo) 120cm by 150cm (4ft x 5ft); large floor rug (saden) 180cm by 275cm (6ft x 9ft); and pillar rug (kathum) 90cm by 180cm (3ft x 6ft).

Some utilitarian pieces, for example saddle rugs (makden and masho) and chair-seat and back rugs (thigyarbya) are also woven, as are animal forehead decorations (tekheb).

BOTTOM RIGHT Small Tibetan sitting mat (circa 1910) displaying auspicious animals.

BELOW Tibetan pillar rug (circa 1900), sewn to form a tube was hung at a temple entrance.

CHAPTER THREE

THE RUGS OF CENTRAL ASIA

The rugs and weavings of Central Asia are tribal and nomadic, with the exception of Beshir rugs. The principal rug-weaving tribes were the Turkoman, Kazakhs, Uzbeks, Kirghiz and Karakalpaks.

Turkoman rugs

Turkoman rugs come in many different shades of red with all-over patterns of polygons called guls.

The shade of red, shape of gul and the particular motifs incorporated help to distinguish between the rugs of the principal tribal divisions of Teke, Salor, Saryk, Yomud, Chodor, Ersari and Beshir.

Types of weaving Rugs for the floor; large storage bags (juval) 60–90cm by 120–180cm (2–3ft x 4–6ft); shallow storage bags (torba) 30cm by 90–150cm (1ft x 3–5ft); small bags (mafrash) 30cm by 60cm (1ft x 2ft);

LEFT This pattern (circa 1890) is from an unknown trial group, but five- or six-sided asmalyks are usually attributed to the Yomuds. An asmalyk decorated a bridal camel.

donkeybags (khorjin); rugs to hang over yurt entrance (ensi) 120cm by 180cm (4ft x 6ft); rugs, shaped like an inverted 'U' to hang inside the entrance (kaplyk); tent bands of various widths; pentagonal or heptagonal weavings as wedding trappings for the bridal camel (asmalyk); and bride rugs 90cm by 90cm (3ft x 3ft).

The gul is the principal pattern and it takes different shapes and sizes. Following are some of the guls used by the tribes.

Teke gul Rounded and connected vertically and horizontally by blue lines.
Salor or turret gul Found on the carpets of the Teke, Saryk and Ersari tribes, it has triangular projections around the edge.
Gul-i-gul Used in many forms on Salor, Ersari and Saryk rugs.

Typical Salor juval (circa 1840) exhibits the juval gul with small diamond secondary guls, with some detail woven in silk. The skirt or elem shows a stylized plant motif.

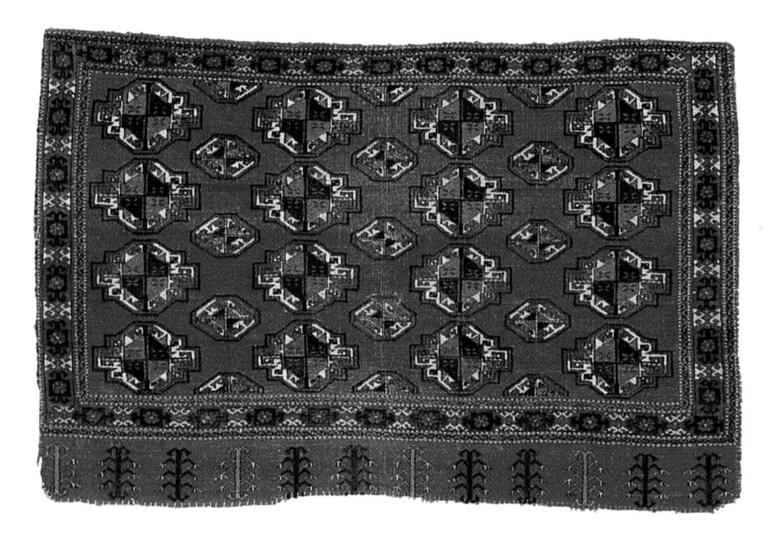

Dyrnak gul Diamond-shaped with hook projections.
Juval or saryk gul Similar to the Teke gul, but not connected by lines.
Kepse gul Diamond-shaped gul with bi-coloured, serrated panels on the edges. It is known to be used only by the Yomud.
Tauk nuska gul With two small animals in each gul quarter, it is one of the most widely used and appears on the main carpets of most tribes.
Ertmen gul Found primarily on Chodor carpets.
Chemche, kurbage, Memling, erre and sagdak These secondary guls used by many tribes.

Non-gul and floral patterns are found on the field and borders of rugs called Beshir. These are not considered to be nomadic. Many of the patterns are Persianate or derived from textiles such as ikats.

Colours are important in distinguishing between the weavings of different tribes. The reds used cover a wide spectrum – for example, there are brown-red, rust-red, mid-reds, purple-red and purple. The blues used are mostly very dark blue or blue-black; mid- and light-blues are rare. Yellow occurs in many shades from light to very strong. Blue-green is found frequently as a secondary colour. Natural white and brown wool is also used.

Technical features used in determining a tribal attribution are: type of major and secondary gul (on main carpets); type of knot; knot density; warp and weft wool colour, warp depression, colour of red; edge finish and special features.

TURKOMAN AND BALUCHI WEAVING

Turkoman weavings were produced mainly in the three Soviet states of Turkmenistan, Karakalpakstan and Uzbekistan. The primary influences on the life and culture of these war-like regions have been Mongolian and Turkish, and many of the motifs found in Turkoman weavings can be traced to these sources.

The origins of existing Turkoman weaving are a matter of some controversy. The traditional view was that the Turkomans, essentially nomadic people, used their carpets as functional objects and for no other purpose; the weavings thus had only a short life. Recent scholarship, however, disputes this, for it now seems clear that the Turkomans did regard their weavings with some respect, and wove not only pieces for their tents but also for urban dwellings.

Turkoman weavings have a predominant colour-scheme of red, red-brown and red-blue; the principal motif is the gul (sometimes written as ghul, ghol or gol), an octagon or a variant on the octagon, containing other, smaller motifs, that may represent a highly-formalized flower. This stylized motif is quite likely to have close associations with one specific Turkoman tribe or to a sub-tribe (the Beshir, Kizil-Ayak and Arabatchi, and Karakalpak). After 1884, many Turkoman tribes also set up bases in Afghanistan.

RIGHT A turned-under top edge and a patterned kelim designate this as a Karakalpak ensi (circa 1890).

Baluchi tribes

Like the Turkomans, the Baluchi tribes generally wove small pieces and bags for use in desert living. A poor people, their main weaving area straddles the Persian-Afghan border for some hundreds of kilometres, their main market-place the town of Torbat in the north, 100 kilometres (60 miles) south of Meshed.

Baluchi wool is especially soft, and the colours are deep and rich. There is no specific Baluchi design, except that they are fond of Tree of Life motifs. The primary influence on their weaving and their designs and patterns is distinctly Turkoman.

Tribal styles

RIGHT This Teke main carpet (circa 1850) displays the Teke gul.

Teke rugs have the Teke gul; an asymmetric knot open to the right; a knot density of over 150 per 6.5 centimetres square (1 inch square); mainly white wool warps; warps on one level. They are a bright mid-range red, with overcast edges; and a short, velvety texture.

RIGHT Yomud ensi (circa 1870) with dark purple-red contrasting to a bright red. Ensi designs are directional and have elems at the bottom.

Salor rugs exhibit the Salor, juval and gul-i-guls; an asymmetric knot open to the left; a knot density of over 150 per 6.5 centimetres square (1 inch square); white wool warps; deep warp depression; mostly bright, rich reds; red and blue selvedge; and minor use of pink-red silk.

BELOW Saryk main carpet (circa 1870) with juval (Saryk) gul and 'X' main border pattern.

Saryk rugs have juval, Salor and gul-i-guls; a symmetric knot; a knot density over 100 knots per 6.5 centimetres square (1 inch square); mainly white wool warps; depressed warps; rust, mahogany- and purple-reds; red and blue selvedge in early rugs, overcast edges in later ones; and a short pile with white cotton and pink-red silk.

Yomud rugs have the dyrnak, kepse and tauk nuska guls; both symmetric and asymmetric knots; a knot density of over 100 knots per 6.5 centimetres square (1 inch square); white to grey wool warps; warps mostly on one level; all types of reds. The edges are selvedge and overcast. There is a white-ground main border; a curled leaf pattern for the main border; and cotton or part-cotton wefts.

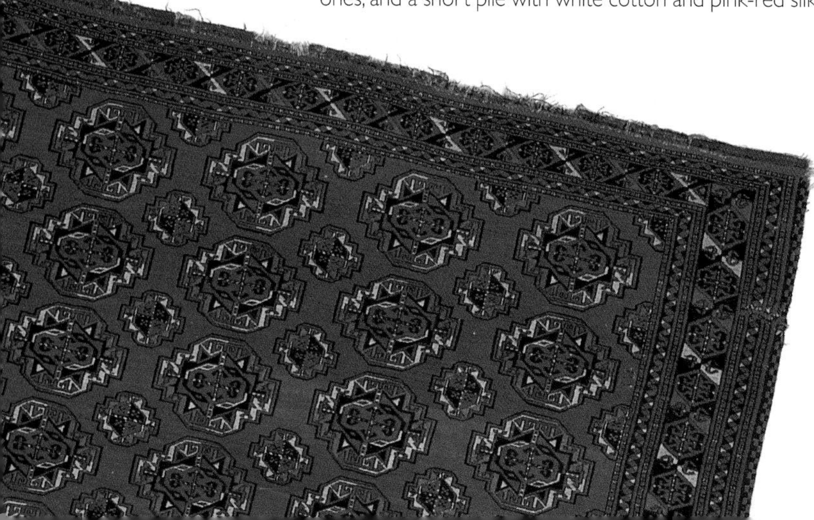

Ersari rugs have the gul-i-gul and tauk nuska guls; an asymmetric knot mostly open to the right; a knot density of over 70 knots per 6.5 centimetres square (1 inch square). The warps are white to grey and they are on one level or slightly depressed; bright to rust-reds; brown selvedge. Yellow is sometimes used as a minor colour; loose, heavy handle; and lustrous wool.

LEFT The border pattern and colours in this Uzbek rug (circa 1900) are typical of an undefined but specific group of Uzbek weavers

Beshir rugs are distinctive because of the use of non-gul patterns; asymmetric knots mostly open to the right; a knot density over 50 knots per 6.5 centimetres square (1 inch square); white, grey and brown warps on one level. The colours used are medium and rust-reds; brown, blue and red selvedge and much yellow.

BELOW Uzbeck julhir, or sleeping rug, (circa 1880) consists of four strips sewn together.

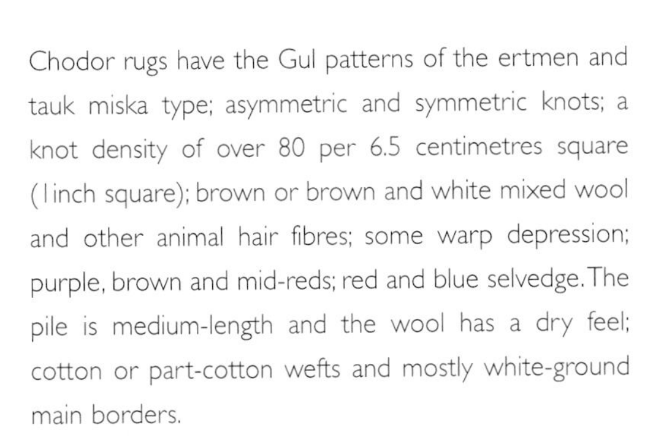

Chodor rugs have the Gul patterns of the ertmen and tauk miska type; asymmetric and symmetric knots; a knot density of over 80 per 6.5 centimetres square (1inch square); brown or brown and white mixed wool and other animal hair fibres; some warp depression; purple, brown and mid-reds; red and blue selvedge. The pile is medium-length and the wool has a dry feel; cotton or part-cotton wefts and mostly white-ground main borders.

ABOVE Uzbek rug (circa 1900) from an undefined group of weavers, bears a pattern derived from a type of Central Asian silk fabric called ikat.

Turkoman flatweaves

Least-known of the Turkoman weavings, flatweaves served specific functions and have a unique design repertoire. Following are some of the notable types:

Main carpets Yomud, Teke and Ersari tribes produced large flatwoven rugs. The most common technique used is cicim with a simple four-part kotshak design within a lattice. The weave varies from coarse in Ersari pieces to very fine in Yomud and Teke ones. Another design is horizontal bands with mihrab or arch shapes in them. These are attributed to the Yomud and Teke.

Juvals, torbas and donkeybags Memling gul used on juvals, with small, all-over repeats used on small bags.

Tent bands Patterns woven in pile on a flatweave ground, or weft- or warp-faced patterns.

Kelims Dovetail and slit tapestry techniques are used in the examples attributed to the Yomud and Ersari.

Other nomadic weavings

The Uzbeks, Karakalpaks, Kirghiz and Kazakhs rugs are all nomadic in style and were woven without commercial consideration.

Most of the tribes used their wool for the production of felts instead of woven articles. Many woven articles have patterns directly related to felt patterns.

But what woven examples have made it to the West exhibit coarsely knotted weavings and the Memling gul is a pattern frequently seen. Some of these tribes wove a type of rug, unique to them, called a julhir. This served as a sleeping rug. Julhirs are woven as one piece or constructed of several strips sewn together.

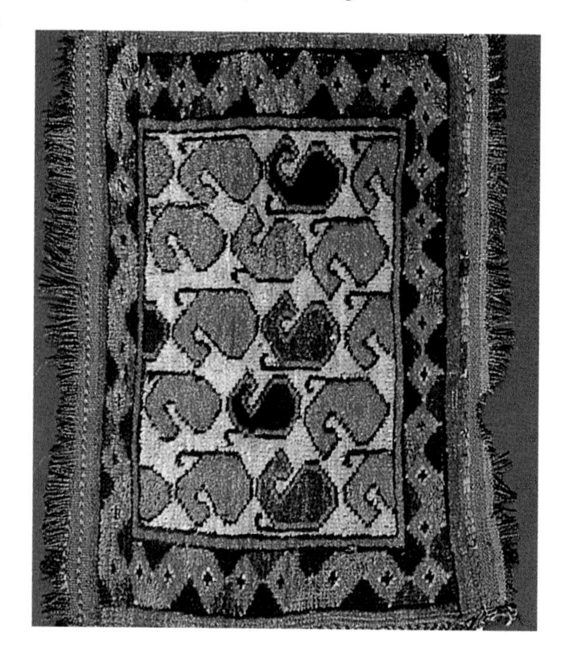

RIGHT Displaying an unusual boteh pattern in bold, simple colours is an Uzbek torba (circa 1880).

CHAPTER FOUR

THE RUGS OF IRAN

Iranian rugs cover the entire range of types more comprehensively than those of any other country. For centuries village and city weaving in Iran has been of a commercial nature, though most of the country's nomadic and tribal rugs were unaffected by this. To understand Iranian rugs it is best to consider them from the point of view of the weaver's lifestyle.

LEFT A Yalamah rug (circa 1950) with typical medallion type.

City rugs

Except for the central region where several cities are renowned for their carpets, one city dominates the field in each of the north, south and east regions – Tabriz, Kerman and Mashhad.

Tabriz

This city has been a centre of weaving for centuries and it was largely from here that the great carpet boom of the nineteenth century began. All types, sizes and designs are woven here. Wool and silk are used in Tabriz. Most rugs are woven on cotton foundations (with the exception of silk rugs) and both symmetric and asymmetric knots are used. Tabriz rugs have a characteristic feel. If the hand is placed under the rug on the back, stiff, bristle-like hairs can be felt.

The most collectable rugs from Tabriz are of silk, especially Heriz silk rugs. Although the patterns and designs of Heriz silk rugs are varied, one constant feature is the presence of unreconciled borders. If the borders are reconciled, the rug is known as a Tabriz rug. Silk rug

ABOVE In colour and design, this Tabriz rug (circa 1900) is representative. Light colours and delicate patterning are effective in the abrashed field.

designs include prayer rugs, pictorials and medallions. Other Tabriz rugs with wool pile in these same patterns are also collected.

RIGHT A wonderful example of a Lavar Kerman prayer rug (circa 1850) showing realistically-drawn trees, flowers and birds.

Kerman

Located in the south, Kerman rugs are among the finest woven in the country. The most desired of the Kerman rugs is called Ravar or Lavar, the name of a town nearby. These rugs were noted for their fine weave, their rich and vibrant cochineal-red, ivory and gold colours and elegant medallions. Kerman rugs were woven mainly in carpet and rug sizes, with most collectors favouring and actively seeking out the prayer rugs.

Mashhad

Located in the the north-west and, except for one type, its rugs are of average quality. A cochineal-red colour is the dominant red used.

BELOW A Kerman saddle cover (circa 1880) with boteh pattern that was produced by city weavers.

Emogli rugs are usually woven of silk and were the finest workshop rugs made in Mashhad. They are almost always red with a dense, floral arabesque design; medallions are sometimes used. Some rugs were made on cotton foundations.

Central Iran

Several of the most famous rug production centres are located in central Iran. One – Kashan – has been a weaving centre for centuries; the others are relative newcomers to the field.

Kashan is the oldest and most famous of the Central Iranian cities. In overall quality it has been the most consistent producer this century. Many designs are used, but medallions have always been a forté of Kashan designers. Small rugs and Tree of Life prayer rugs are the focus of collectors.

Isfahan, Nain and Qum are newcomers to the high-quality, city rug group and are best-known for small rugs. Silk, in whole or in part, figures prominently. Except for all-silk carpets, they are woven on cotton warps and wefts with asymmetric knots. In creating a carpet industry in these places, designers were inspired by the sixteenth century designs of Shah Abbas, one of the rulers of Persia during its golden age of art.

PERSIAN RUGS

As more Persian carpets come onto the market in the West than any other type, the following list – albeit very incomplete – of names that a prospective purchaser is likely to encounter will prove useful.

Afshar Tribal rugs from south of Kerman.

Ainabad or Bibikabad Kurdish rugs woven in Ainabad.

Arak (Sultanabad) Trade name for carpets marketed in that town.

Bakhtiari Semi-nomadic rugs woven near Isfahan.

Herez Used also as a general trade name.

Birjand Trade name for coarse rugs marketed through Meshed.

Bozchelu (Borchelu) Kurdish village rugs of Bozchelu, marketed through Hamadan.

Derghezin Kurdish rugs woven in this district and marketed through Hamadan.

Dorukhsh (Dorosh) Produced fine pieces in the early nineteenth-century; modern pieces poor.

Feraghan (Ferahan) Generic name for fine Kurdish rugs woven in and around this area.

Herez A major weaving centre located in north-west Persia.

Isfahan For modern pieces, denotes rugs woven in the town itself or rugs of a certain quality marketed in Meshed, but not woven in Isfahan.

Joshaqan Rugs woven from 1700 in this town, or name given to rugs exhibiting particular designs.

Karaja (Karadia) Rugs show Caucasian influence.

Khorassan Generic name, much abused in the trade, for weavings from eastern province of Persia.

Kum City with modern weaving industry.

Kurdish Generic name for north-west Persia tribal type that defy specific nomenclature.

Laver Kerman Trade name for old type Kerman rug.

Mahal Trade name for a quality of rug woven around Arak.

Mehreban Used by the trade to describe rugs of particular quality not woven in the Mehreban area.

Mosul Trade name for coarse rug, Kurdish-type marketed in Hamadan.

Petag Persian Carpet Company, active 1900-1930.

Senneh Fine weavings but name misused in the trade.

Serab or Sarab Now a trade name for some Kashgai weavings.

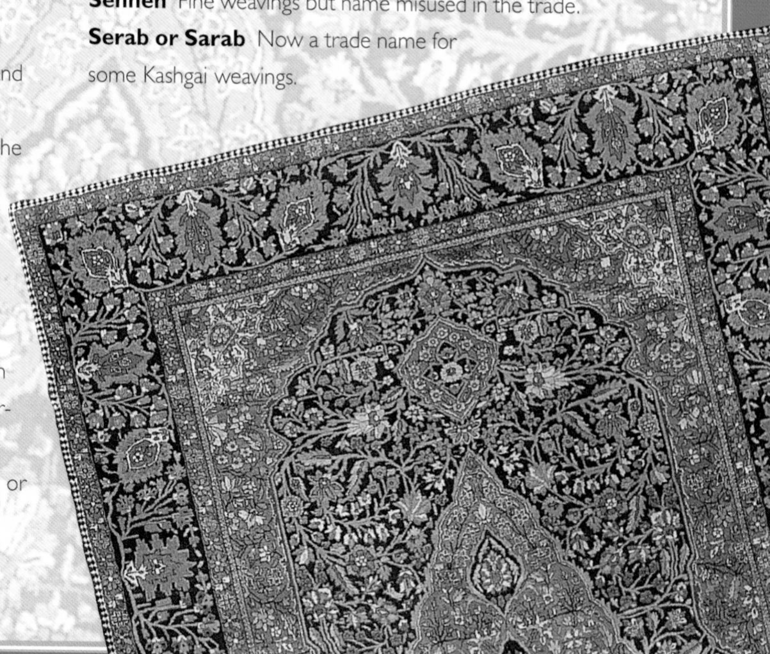

RIGHT Typical Kashan rug (circa 1900) with medallion and floral patterning.

RIGHT A Heriz Bakshaish rug (circa 1880) with unusual medallions.

BELOW Though the colours are typical of Heriz carpets (circa 1910), the small medallion with large anchor pendant is not.

Village rugs

Some villages use designs and patterns in their rugs that have remained unchanged by commercial influences; these are the ones which are collected.

North-western villages

These villages orbit the city of Tabriz, and the rugs woven use the Turkish knot.

Heriz has given its name to a group of rugs, mostly room size, though with a decorative purpose, that have a distinctive character. They are also known as Serapi, Bakshaish, Ahar and Karaja. Few small rugs were made, and these appeal to collectors. They have medallions and all-over patterns and are woven with cotton warps and wefts.

Sarab produces a distinctive group mostly of runners. These have wide outer borders in natural camel hair or wool dyed the colour of camel hair. The field has series of large, connected medallions. Pinks and blues are used in the patterns, which are geometric and floral. They have mostly wool warps and wefts.

West Iran

West Iran Is the most prolific rug-weaving region. The commercial rugs of Hamadan, Sarouk, Lilihan and Saraband are from here, as are the Senneh, Bijar and Chahar Mahal rugs. Other village rugs of note originate from Maslaghan, Malayer, Sarouk and Ferahan.

Maslaghan produced a medallion-design rug that is unlike any other Hamadan rug. Most are about 120cm

BELOW Serab rug (circa 1910) with distinctive colours and several connected medallions.

by 180cm (4ft x 6ft) and single wefted. They are woven with the symmetric knot and have cotton warps with either cotton or wool wefts. The large, angularly-lobed medallion and field are patterned with small designs. The ground colour of the medallion contrasts sharply with the colour of the field. The borders are narrow. The result is a dramatic and bold design.

Malayers have a single weft, symmetric knot and most are about 120cm by 180cm (4ft x 6ft) and have all-over and medallion designs. The boteh appears frequently. Malayer, Sarouk and Ferahan all have cotton warps and wefts. Some describe a Malayer, as a Senneh rug without the characteristic feel.

Sarouks come in carpet and rug sizes, with arabesque-filled medallion designs the hallmark. Red, blue and white are the predominant colours with occasional greens. They are finely and tightly woven.

Ferahans have all-over patterns, particularly the herati; and medallions are slightly angular. They are noted for a particular shade of green that is corrosive.

South Iran

Productions developed for commercial markets from the settled villages of Abadeh and Yalemeh date from the middle of the twentieth century. They were once common in the marketplace.

Abadehs take their patterns and designs from the Qashqai. The difference is that they are woven with cotton warp and wefts, and the latter is often dyed blue. Rugs were no larger than 180cm by 275cm (6ft x 9ft).

LEFT An unusual Sarouk carpet (circa 1910) with architectural 'pillars' supporting the arches on the field. The abrash creates a three-dimensional illusion.

BELOW The animals at each end and the random flowers show the weaver's individual touch on this Malayer rug (circa 1900).

Yalemehs are more closely allied with the Khamseh patterns. The small rugs have multiple medallions ringed with latchhooks; the same medallions are arranged in a grid of borders in larger rugs and carpets. They are woven with wool warps and wefts, although cotton was also used for wefts.

East Iran

The one village of note is Dorokhsh. Most common rugs are 120cm by 180cm (4ft x 6ft) and the boteh is the most common pattern. Red-orange is a characteristic colour. They have an asymmetric knot and usually a single border.

TOP RIGHT Like all Kurdish rugs, this one (circa 1850) shows infinite pattern and design variety. Gold and yellow are often the dominant colours in Kurdish rugs.

Tribal and nomadic rugs

These rugs are produced by several ethnic groups, including the Kurds, Bakhtiari and Luri, Qashqai and Khamseh, Afshar, Baluchi and Shahsavan, some of which lead both settled and nomadic lifestyles.

Kurdish rugs

Kurds inhabit Turkey, Iran, Iraq and Syria, but in Iran they are a major weaving group. Weavers use a wide range of patterns, types and styles. The Kurds are master colourists, and their rugs exhibit possibly the finest carpet wools of those of any nomadic tribes. Kurdish wool is durable, lustrous and highly-receptive to dyes.

Knot type Symmetric.
Warp and weft fibres Mostly wool, with some cotton. Warps are mostly white wool, but they may be mixed with brown. Wefts are usually brown, although some are red.
Edge and end finishes Selvedge and overcast edge, and kelims – some with stripes – from 2.5cm (1in)
Colours Yellow and both natural and corrosive browns were used.

RIGHT Typical of Jaf Kurd weaving is this bagface (circa 1920) with its offset knotting, design and colouring. The top is dovetail and slit tapestry weave.

Kurdish village rugs are primarily identified with the areas of Hamadan, Senneh and Bijar. Hamadan is one of the largest commercial weaving areas, but its rugs are not generally collected. The rugs of Senneh and Bijar (located to the north of Senneh) are produced commercially, but they are also highly collectable and their characteristics distinguish them from all other rugs.

Sennehs are among the finest woven village rugs from west-central Iran. They are single-wefted, with a short pile and no warp depression. The back of a Senneh rug feels like fine sandpaper. When a Senneh rug is not as finely woven as expected, it is called a Senneh Kurd.

Bijars are among the sturdiest carpets, small rugs and bags woven; they have depressed warps and are very compact. They have great design and pattern variety. Those of lesser quality are referred to as Bijar Kurd.

Veramin, a town south of Tehran, is noted for a particular group of nomadic weavings. Most of them are bagfaces with blue fields and Turkoman guls.

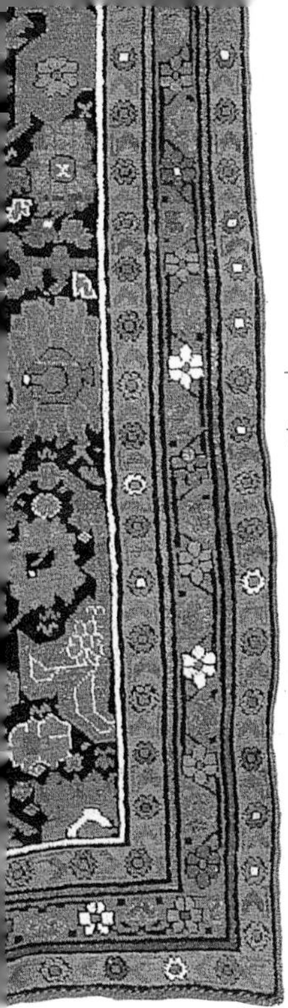

Bakhtiari and Luri rugs

The Bakhtiari and Luri tribes live in the mountains and plains east of Isfahan to the Iraqi border. Bakhtiari rugs are of both nomadic and village types, and Luri rugs are of the nomadic type. The nomadic pieces are mostly large bags, donkeybags and kelims. The Bakhtiaris also owned villages in the area of their summer camp grounds in Chahar Mahal. These two groups – the Bakhtiari and Luri, and the Chahar Mahal are considered separately.

The technical characteristics of nomadic Bakhtiari and Luri rugs are listed below.

Knot type Symmetric.

Warp and weft fibres Wool, with some use of goat hair or cotton. Warps in Luri rugs are mostly natural browns, some mixed with white; in Bakhtiaris they are white with some natural brown mixed. Wefts in both are natural browns or red.

Edge and end finishes Edges mostly overcast in dark brown wool or goat hair. End finish may be a 2.5–7.5cm (1–3in) kelim weave in natural colour or with stripes.

Colours Dark blues predominate; reds are light in tone; and yellows strong.

Technical features For many large bags white cotton is used; bag bottoms are woven in pile.

The Chahar Mahals are large carpets and rugs. The most common pattern is an all-over one of squares or lozenge-shapes with various trees and flowers in them. Their technical characteristics are:

Knot type symmetric.

Warp and weft fibres cotton, some blue-wefted.

Edge and end finishes overcast in black wool, and kelim weave of 2.5––5cm (1–2in).

Technical features Inscriptions are frequently found in these rugs.

BELOW Deeply saturated reds and blues, soft and lustrous wool identifies this Veramin bagface (circa 1900).

Qashqai and Khamseh rugs

The Qashqai and Khamseh tribes live in south-eastern Iran around the city of Shiraz. Their rugs have similar features. Their weavings are primarily small and area-size rugs and they also produce many bags and utilitarian trappings. The patterns are mainly geometric and include animal, floral and human forms as filler elements. The technical characteristics are listed below.

BELOW A rare Khamseh saddle cover (circa 1880) with slits for the pommel and cantle

Knot type Asymmetric and symmetric.

Warp and weft fibres Wool

Edge and end finishes Qashqai are overcast mostly in two colours of wool; Khamseh overcast or selvedged in dyed wool or natural brown. Kelim weave with twined or brocaded stripes.

Colours Notable are bright reds, shades of blue, good green, and gold as a minor colour.

Technical features Many rugs have two or more narrow end borders with alternating dark blue and white squares.

Qashqai patterns and designs include a three-medallion type and repeated all-over patterns with diagonal colouration. They are generally more tightly-woven than Khamseh rugs.

Many of the Khamseh designs include a distinctive 'chicken' of vertical ribbons in white and dark blue. Most Khamseh rugs have a loose, pliable feel.

Afshar rugs

Most of the Afshar rugs are small, but some are carpets. Some bags and utilitarian pieces were also woven.

Afshar rugs divide into two groups, depending on whether wool is used for warps and wefts. They feature both geometric and floral patterns in medallion and all-over designs.

Knot types Asymmetric and symmetric.

Warp and weft fibres White wool, occasionally mixed brown, for warps; wefts wool, mostly orange-red or pink. Some warp depression. Cotton used for warps and/or wefts in later pieces.

Edge and end finishes Overcast with dyed wool. Kelim of 2.5–15cm (1–6in).

Colours Rust reds with a yellow undertone are used; a salmon-orange secondary colour is also an identifying feature.

Technical feature Afshar wool is dry to touch and has low lustre.

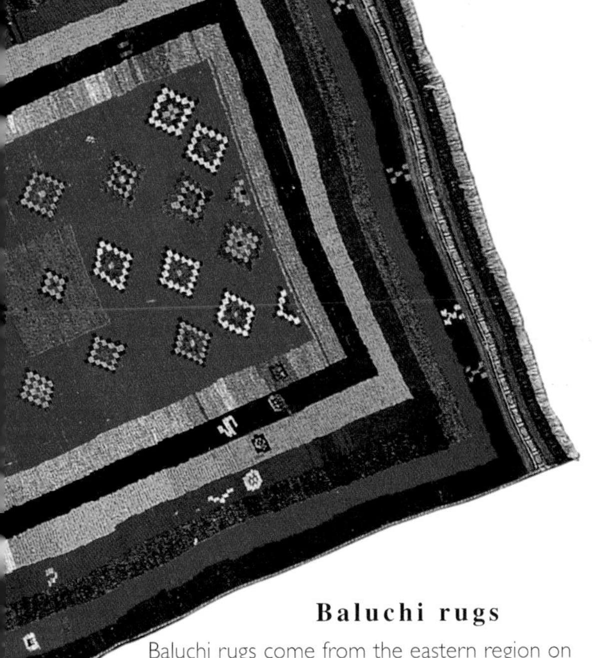

TOP LEFT Reminiscent of an abstract painting is this Qashqai gabbeh rug (circa 1850), with its saturated colour begging for some response from the viewer.

Baluchi rugs

Baluchi rugs come from the eastern region on the Afghanistan and Turkmenistan borders. Most rugs are small and many are in prayer rug format.

They exhibit one of the darkest palettes in red and blue combined with dark brown and white outlining. Natural camel hair is common. The patterns are both floral and geometric. Large numbers of bags also produced.

Knot type Asymmetric open left, a few open right and some symmetric.

Warp and weft fibres Warps are white wool; wefts are dark brown wool. Note that newer Baluchi rugs from Iran have cotton warps and wefts.

Edge and end finishes Selvedge in brown wool or goat hair. Ends 2.5–25 cm (1–10 in) kelim in coloured stripes, patterned with brocade techniques or simply left plain.

Technical features Soft, lustrous wool and brilliant blue hues.

LEFT Because of size, the filler animals are poorly drawn on this Khamseh bagface (circa 1900).

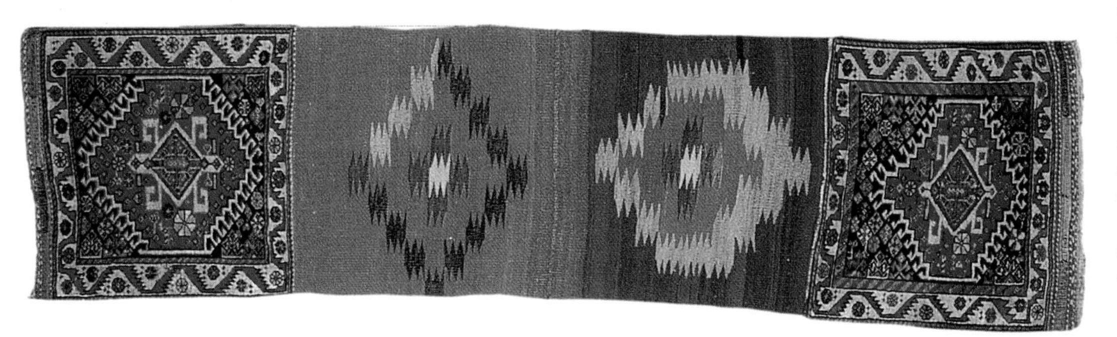

LEFT An opened-out Qashqai donkeybag (circa 1880) shows a particularly dramatic pattern.

Shahsavan rugs

Most are flatweaves, and the patterns are geometric and in a wide variety of colours. Most weavings are storage bags, floor kelims and covers. The patterns and designs are among the most interesting of all flatweaves.

RIGHT The arms on this Shahsavan horse cover would be secured around the horse's chest. This example (circa 1900) is unusual in that it was woven in one piece.

Iranian flatweaves

Flatweaves are made by all of the nomadic weavers of Iran and by many of the village weavers. Each has its own characteristic features, patterns and techniques.

Most Shahsavan flatweaves are woven using the soumak technique. Today most exist as bagfaces. They have an exceptional and interesting design repertoire and make for great collecting.

Qashqai flatweaves are woven in sizes of about 180cm by 305cm (6ft x 10ft) in slitweave and dovetail tapestry. They were made as floor rugs and coverings. The simple abstract design of many Qashqai kelims appeals to those who like modern art.

Kurdish, Baluchi and Luri/Bakhtiari flatweaves are known, but have not yet become popular. Kurdish flatweaves are still waiting to be thoroughly studied. The flatweaves of the Baluchi are even darker than the rugs and are difficult to appreciate, but are among the most complex and challenging. Luri/Bakhtiari flatweaves enjoyed a burst of interest in the 1970s.

Of village flatweaves, the two most notable are Sennehs and Bijars. Senneh kelims are the finest ever woven by Oriental weavers. The best, because of their fineness, are those from before the First World War. Later examples were woven on coarser cotton warps. The boteh and herati figure prominently as patterns. The finest examples have multi-coloured silk warps.

CHAPTER FIVE

THE RUGS OF THE CAUCASUS

The rugs of the Caucasus are essentially village rugs, and their bold colours, geometric designs and folk art features appeal to most people. They are easily divided, according to design and weave characteristics, into those from the western and those from eastern Caucasus. This division is generally between rugs with large patterns and relatively coarse weave, and those with small patterns and fine weave.

Types of weaving Most are no larger than 180cm by 275cm (6ft x 9ft) which is a reflection of their village origins. There are many prayer rugs about 90cm x 150cm (3ft x 5ft). Utilitarian pieces are mostly donkeybags and covers. Large rugs were made in workshops in a few cities. Many runners were woven.

Patterns Geometric and floral patterns are used. In the western area, large geometric medallions predominate. In the eastern area smaller patterns are typical.

Colours Red, blue, yellow, green and white in pure tones are standard.

Technical characteristics The following chart shows the differences between rugs of the region.

	WESTERN	EASTERN
Type of knot	Symmetric	Symmetric
Density of weave	40-100 knots per 6.5 square centimetre (1 square in)	80-200 knots per 6.5 square centimetre (1 square in)
Pile height	Medium to high	Short to medium
Warp material colour	Wool, white and mixed brown	Wool, white, few mixed
Weft material colour	Wool, natural and dyed	Wool and cotton, natural
Number of wefts	3 or more	2 rarely more
Edge finish	Wool selvedge, some dyed	Some blue wool, some cotton

ABOVE A typical example of a Karachov Kazak rug (circa 1890).

TOP RIGHT This Kuba rug (circa 1880) is special in that at the beginning end of the rug the weaver intended two rows of guls, but had to stop because of lack of room. Such a 'misjudgment' is a sure sign that the rug's origins are village or nomadic.

Areas of production

Caucasian weaving from the last two centuries is very complex. Although there are inevitably some cultural and ethnic overlaps, it is possible to divide the Caucasus into the ten main weaving areas of: Kazak, Karabagh, Gendje, Talish, Moghan, Shirvan, Baku, Kuba, Daghestan and Derbend.

It should be noted, however, that the generic name Kazak is often applied to a wide variety of Caucasian rugs not necessarily woven in the Kazak district.

LEFT This Chichi Shirvan rug (circa 1880) has an atypical border of Kufic script.

RIGHT The large 'ram's horn' (or latchhook) patterns in the field are identifiers of Perepedils. The border patterns are found on many types of Kuba rugs. Except for indigo, this Perepedil Kuba rug (circa 1880) was dyed with early synthetic dyes. They faded to pale colours or were chemically treated.

CAUCASIAN WEAVING

Caucasian carpets come from an area between the Black Sea and the Caspian Sea. Although many of the carpets of the so-called 'north-west Persian Caucasian' group were probably woven inside the present borders of Iran in the region between the towns of Tabriz in the south and Erivan (now called Yerevan) in the north, the majority were woven in, and north of, the regions that used to be called Armenia, Karabagh, Kazak, Moghan and Shirvan, regions now incorporated into Armenia and Azerbaijan. For the purposes of any discussion of Caucasian weaving, however, these older names must be retained.

Barbarism and a cultural melting-pot

The carpets of the Caucasus mirror the ethnography of their creators. Until the Russian conquests of the late eighteenth and nineteenth centuries, the area had been for over 800 years a melting-pot and a ceaseless battle-ground. Arabs, Tartars, Turks, Mongols, Persians, Russians and others were constantly seeking to make the region theirs. Both the cultural mix and the barbarism are displayed in Caucasian carpet design.

The earliest Caucasian weavings are the dragon rugs – though heated debate surrounds this issue – that are thought to be based on Persian prototypes involving stylized animals, sometimes in combat, which then became assimilated into the four Caucasian standard forms. The earliest is least stylized, and has a lozenge-diaper surround of serrate leaves. In the second type, stylization of the dragon is augmented and the lozenge diaper is disintegrating. The third is a further stage of this progression. And in the fourth type, which dates from about 1750 to 1850, the format has become pretty well geometric.

The Caucasians also produced floral rugs, generally in Kuba, to the north. Again, the earliest are based on Persian designs, with lattices. But there are also tree rugs, and a third type involving rows of individual palmettes, flowers or leaves.

RIGHT The Lesghi star – the three large stellate medallions – are common in Caucasus rugs, and Shirvan rugs are no exception.

RIGHT Fachralo Kazak prayer rug (circa 1880) displaying the mihrab arch (the five-sided band extending between the main borders) inside a dramatic leaf and calyx border.

Rugs of the Eastern Caucasus

These rugs have strong colours and are finely-woven, with intricate repeat patterns. The area is divided into three: rugs from the northern section are known as Kubas; south of it the rugs are called Shirvan; Baku rugs come from the region south of the city of Baku.

Kuba rugs

Kuba rugs exhibit a great variety of patterns. They have wool wefts and typically more than 100 knots per 6.5 centimetres square (1 inch square). Many have blue wool selvedge and blue soumak weaving on the ends. They have a higher pile than Shirvan rugs. Many shades of blue and salmon-red are used. Several of the better known designs are listed below.

Chichi Pattern of geometric forms in rows including the Memling gul, and the main border is distinctive. Has an overall greenish colouration.

Perepedil Series of 'ram's horn' patterns in the centre and edge of the field.

Seishour or St. Andrew's Cross Large, repeated cross design in the field that is often white and blue. The main border is a blue and white pattern called the Georgian border. Rugs with realistically-drawn roses are also called Seishour.

Alpan Similar to Star Kazak but rendered smaller on small rugs and runners. Alpan rugs frequently exhibit very intense yellows.

Flower or snowflake Medium-sized rosette arranged in diagonally-coloured rows.

Flower lattice All-over lattice pattern with flowers within the lozenge spaces.

Shirvan rugs

These have cotton wefts and overcast edges, which may be cotton or wool. Pile is clipped short. Several of the better-known designs are listed on the next page.

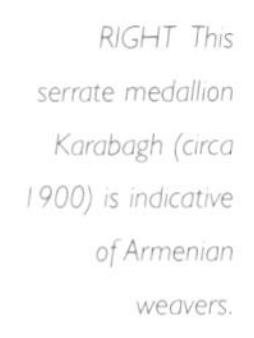

RIGHT This serrate medallion Karabagh (circa 1900) is indicative of Armenian weavers.

Lesghi star Large, geometric, eight-pointed star with stepped edges.

Boteh Pattern woven in many variations and with interesting colour usage.

Garden Series of linked rectangles and octagons, giving the impression of the lay-out of a Persian garden.

Bijov Interlocking palmette and bracket patterns in an ascending arrangement.

Akstafa Large eight-pointed medallions alternating with large birds. The main border is usually white with large geometric patterns.

Baku, Talish, Lenkoran and Moghan rugs

These come from south of Baku and while they share a geographic region, they differ structurally.

Baku Standard design has an ivory central medallion on a blue field filled with botehs. The main border is ivory or pale blue with alternating rosettes and birds.

Talish Wide runners with plain, mostly blue fields. The main border is white, with an alternating pattern of one large and four small rosettes.

Lenkoran Structurally similar to Talish, but they are more coarsely woven and have a distinctive medallion.

Moghan Memling gul and a latchhook diamond are the most common pattern.

Rugs of the Western Caucasus

The rugs of this region have a reputation for bold patterns, vivid colour and strong designs. The western area is divided into two regions. The rugs from the north are Kazaks; those from the south Karabaghs.

Kazak rugs

These are among the largest woven rugs and they have a long pile and are made of lustrous wool. The wefts are frequently dyed red and the selvedges may be woven in more than one colour. Some of the better-known Kazak designs are listed below.

Star Kazak Large eight-pointed stars alternate with eight-pointed medallions on white ground.

Pinwheel Kazak Red ground with pinwheel medallions; rosette secondary pattern green and white.

Karachov Kazak Large octagonal medallion with chequerboard corners and four small square medallions in each corner of the field.

Shield or Sevan Kazak Large medallion that fills

BELOW Clear colours and simplicity of patterns typify Kazak weaving.

LEFT An elegant example of the shield design on this Kazak rug (circa 1880).

RIGHT The red wefts are typical of Kazak weaving, while the colours, border and medallion shape is clearly Karabagh.

the field. There are three variations of the medallion form.

Lori Pambak Large octagonal medallion with pendant irregular medallions or three large medallions of the same type in different colours.

Three-medallion Kazak Octagon medallion and two stepped medallions of different colours on a red field.

Fachralo Kazak Large six- or ten-sided medallion containing a smaller medallion in a different colour.

Borchalu Kazak Main borders with latchhook patterns and narrow field of small latchhook medallions.

Karabagh rugs

These are not as large as Kazaks and are more rectangular in shape. They may have dyed wefts, but dark brown is typical. The dark weft is used for the kelim ends. The pile is shorter than in Kazaks and a crab border is typical. Some of the better-known designs are listed below.

Sunburst, Cheleberd or Eagle Kazak One to three large-rayed medallions with a cruciform centre.

Cloudband or Kondzoresk One to three octagonal medallions with four pairs of S-shapes in the centre.

Serrate-edge medallion Several, closely-spaced, diamond-shaped medallions on a field.

Genje Rugs with diagonal stripes in different colours. The stripes have botehs or flowers on them.

Shusha and Erivan Patterns for these city rugs are floral and Persianate. A cochineal red is frequently used. Most have cotton wefts and closely-clipped pile.

Lampa Karabagh Series of large and small connected medallions with large birds in the field.

Caucasus flatweaves

Caucasian flatweaves possess many of the same characteristics of colour and design as the rugs. They were woven primarily for use by the weaver as rugs, curtains, room dividers, wrappers and covers, and for agricultural purposes.

Descriptions of the five main types of Caucasus flatweaves follow.

Kelims Wide and narrow horizontal bands with geometric patterns or large palmettes arranged in diagonally coloured rows are the two main designs. Both are about 150–210cm by 245–335cm (5–7ft x 8–11ft).

Soumaks Dragon and three-medallion types are the most common for these large rugs.

Zilis Generally woven in two pieces that were sewn together to form a rug or carpet, the most common pattern is an S-shaped dragon.

Vernehs Patterns are more varied and smaller in size, typically made in one piece.

Cicims Pattern consisting of large squares.

CHAPTER SIX

THE RUGS OF ANATOLIA/TURKEY

The rugs of Anatolia have been known in the West longer than any other type and they appear in the earliest paintings. Because Turkish rug patterns and colours are complex, they are the ones that many collectors learn to appreciate last.

The majority of Turkish rugs are village rugs, and many patterns and designs are associated with specific villages. The city rugs of Turkey are made primarily in and around Istanbul and the cities of Sivas, Izmir, Isparta and Keyseri. These rugs are almost entirely commercially produced and are of little interest to collectors. Silk rugs are woven in the Istanbul area, the best-known and among the finest of their kind being the Herekes.

Nomadic rugs are woven throughout the country, but the greatest numbers come from the eastern region. In Turkey, nomads are known as yörüks, a term also used for nomadic rugs.

Sizes vary, but most items are rug size: that is, smaller than 180cm by 275cm (6ft x 9ft), a reflection of their village and nomadic origins. Carpets are woven primarily in the city workshops. Bags in many sizes and shapes are also woven.

Geometric and floral patterns are frequently combined. Many floral forms have become almost unrecognizable because of the angular drawing. In fine silk rugs, Persianate, floral and arabesque patterns dominate.

Primary and tertiary colours are used, especially yellow, with browns for outlining and major design areas. Use of early synthetic dyes meant that Turkish rugs were synonymous with bleeding and fading. Chrome dyes were substituted in the 1950s and more recently natural dyes have enjoyed a rebirth.

BELOW A fine example of an east Anatolian Yoruk rug (circa 1900) with multiple shades of blue, madder and cochineal; brocaded ends; and a zip-like selvedge.

BELOW Melas rug (circa 1870) showing an unusual flowering plant pattern on the red field.

Many technical characteristics, such as the symmetric knot, are shared by various weaving groups throughout Anatolia. The following table illustrates the ways in which they differ by region. Though, as you will have come to expect in such a complex field, there are always exceptions.

	WEST	CENTRAL	EAST
Warp material colour	Wool, white	Wool, mostly white, some brown mixed	Wool and goat hair, white and brown, mixed
Weft material colour	Wool, red, some brown and white	Wool, brown, white, red, yellow	Wool, mostly brown, blue
Number of wefts	2–4 or more	2–4 or more	2–4 or more
Warp depression	No depression	Occasional depression	No depression
Edge finish	Selvedge, most red and some multicolours	Selvedge, red, yellow and multicolours	Selvedge, multicolours zip weave
End finish	Wide red or striped multicolours	Wide red, yellow or striped multicolours	Wide brown or red blue, striped colours
Special features	Cochineal red	No cochineal red	Cochineal red; braided fringe

Western Anatolia

If any colour scheme predominates, it is red, white and blue. This is especially typical for the area between Çanakkale and Bergama. As you proceed south towards Melas, yellow increases in frequency.

Many of the classical rugs from the Ottoman period that reached the West were woven in this region. The patterns of the so-called Holbein rugs occur in many of the rugs from the Çanakkale-Bergama area. They feature large medallions seen in large-patterned Holbeins or a complex interlocking geometric pattern observed in small-patterned Holbein rugs.

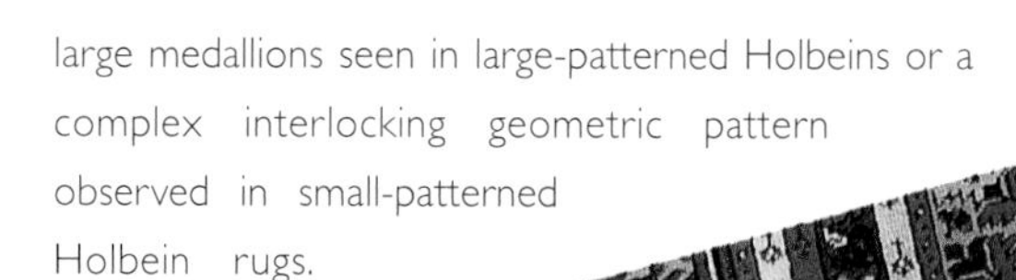

RIGHT Mucur prayer rug (circa 1850) with typical mihrab arch shape.

LEFT Ordu Kurdish kelim (circa 1880) with fringe braided into a flat band. The pattern on the centre band is called elibilinde, meaning 'hands on hips.'

Many of the border patterns echo classical Ushak and Transylvanian rugs. Some western Anatolian rugs prized by collectors sixty to eighty years ago, such as Ghiordes, Kula and Melas, originate from this region.

Central Anatolia

Today the rugs of central Anatolia are of great interest to collectors. As regards pattern, many, especially the Konya rugs, are considered successors to the earliest Anatolian rugs. Their colouring includes a generous use of yellow, but rarely cochineal. Of all Turkish rugs these are the most dramatically coloured.

Ladik and Muçur rugs are still highly prized today. The distinctive prayer rugs are some of the best known. Ladiks are among the most finely-woven village rugs; Muçur prayer rugs are simpler and less floral in patterning. Both have simple, stepped mihrabs (arches) with open fields.

Eastern Anatolia

Produced mainly by Kurds and nomadic groups, rug patterns are almost entirely geometric with edges and ends irregular. Distinctive features are the use of camel hair and a unique selvedge that resembles a zip.

Many designs in large medallion format are found in the rugs from this region. Because they were woven for use in the coldest region of Turkey, the pile was usually left long for insulation, although the weave can also be quite fine.

BELOW This Sivrihisar kelim (circa 1875) is a tour de force as regards colour, design and pattern.

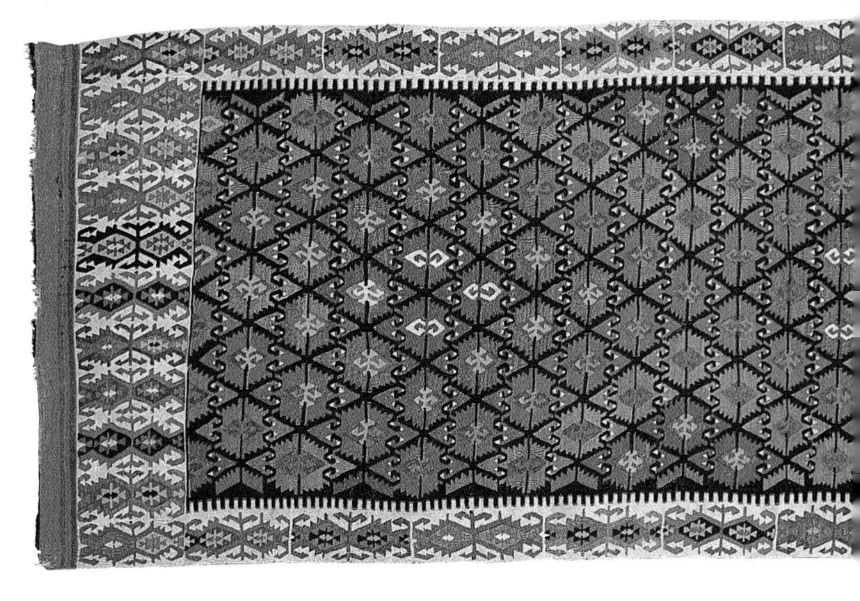

Turkish flatweaves

Flatweaves were made in all parts of Turkey by both village and nomadic weavers. The entire range of techniques is found in Turkish weaving, and the patterns and designs employed are the most extensive of any country. Turkish flatweaves are currently the most popular with collectors, and extremely old examples are considered to be among the finest expression of the weaver's art. Twenty years ago, however, no one was collecting them. This phenomenal reversal is the result of a realization that flatweaves, more than any other weaving from Turkey, fit today's criteria for collecting. The criteria are: they were made for the weaver's use and not for commercial purposes, and they are derivative of the oldest patterns used in weaving.

Turkish flatweaves are categorized by region in much the same way as are pile rugs, except that there is more variety in the functional uses for which they were made.

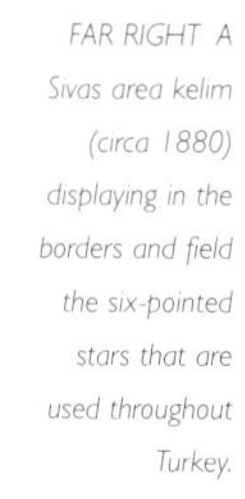

FAR RIGHT A Sivas area kelim (circa 1880) displaying in the borders and field the six-pointed stars that are used throughout Turkey.

RIGHT This is one half of a Konya kelim (circa 1825).

CHAPTER SEVEN

THE NEW COLLECTABLES

In the mid-1960s a rebirth of interest in Oriental rugs began in the United States, spurred on by members of the first American rug society, the Hajji Baba Club, who started focusing on rugs that they believed represented the indigenous culture of the country of origin. This was a shift away from collections based on the court culture that inspired the classical carpets. Thus in the United States and to a lesser degree in Europe, nomadic and tribal rugs became the dominant themes in Oriental rug collecting.

With the new criteria whole classes of rugs became non-collectable. This included city rugs because they were commercial products; rugs that had been chemically treated and painted; rugs utilizing synthetic dyes that ran; and rugs that were believed to be synthetic.

Rugs that collectors early in the century believed were highly desirable were no longer so regarded. Ghiordes, Kula and Bergama rugs, for example, fell in price. Instead rugs that had been bought as good, cheap floor Orientals gradually became the new focus. The Kazaks and Kubas of the Caucasus were recognized for their colour and abstract art qualities. Turkoman rugs were perceived as the finest weaving of nomadic tribes, and Baluchi rugs, which had been loss leaders in rug shops 50 years earlier, were admired for their simplicity of design. Times change and collecting changes; some rugs increase in price, while others, sadly, go down.

For many years, collectors would only consider rugs made before the end of the nineteenth century. This changed in the 1980s with the revival of natural dyeing in Turkey.

DOBAG, the acronym for a project to revive nineteenth-century village patterns and natural dyes, was the principal stimulus for the revival in western Turkey. The rugs acquired the name Ayvaçik, from a principal village of the region. Because of DOBAG's success there are many classes of rugs and flatweaves being woven in western, central and eastern Turkey with naturally-dyed fibres.

ABOVE
This Gabbeh kelim woven in 1993 echoes pattern themes from south Persia.

FAR RIGHT A wonderful depiction of everyday life is told in this pictorial Azeri folklife rug (circa 1993).

BELOW The pattern on this Azeri rug woven in 1993 is derived from Heriz district rugs, though weavers are encouraged to use individual artistic expression.

Iran had been slow to join the natural-dye revival, however a group of handspun yarn and natural dye rugs called Gabbehs have appeared on the market.

The new Gabbeh is woven in the traditional way. There is a slight change in the sizes of the rugs, which are squarer than the originals. Because of their adherence to traditional form, natural dyes and handspun wool, they fit in with the older weaving tradition of the Persian nomadic style. It seems likely that the use of natural dyes will be adapted elsewhere in Iran as the success of the Gabbeh rugs spreads to other regions.

Afghanistan weavers had begun to re-use natural dyes in the 1970s, but the trend was halted by war with Russia. Among refugee weavers in Pakistan efforts were made to revive the use of natural dyes and patterns from nineteenth-century rugs, especially the Ersari and Beshir ones. This effort is in its infancy and production is small. Tibet also has seen a rebirth of natural-dye weaving. The production is centred in workshops in Lhasa and traditional designs are used.

Many collectors continue to avoid rugs with synthetic dyes, but as the price of increasingly fewer nineteenth-century rugs goes up, many find it acceptable to collect rugs from the first half of the twentieth century. Although they have synthetic dyes, they exhibit many of the same qualities of design, colour and use which collectors generally find desirable. Careful selection will result in a fine collection.

The collector

Oriental rugs have been collected since the craft of rug-weaving developed. In the Middle East they were collected as one way of holding wealth. In bad times they were sold as needed. In the western world, it was not until the late nineteenth century that collecting rugs became a pastime on a par with amassing painting and sculpture. The first wave focused entirely on classical carpets woven before 1800. The Fricks, Havemeyers and Rockefellers bought them for their homes in New York and Newport. Ordinary Americans purchased the new rugs from Turkey, the Caucasus and Persia.

In Europe, Baron Thyssen and Calouste Gulbenkian formed two great private collections, and curators in Berlin, London, Vienna and Budapest created the greatest museum collections of fifteenth to eighteenth century Oriental rugs.

This collecting spree lasted until the Depression of the Thirties, and resumed when the Second World War ended and economies began to recover. During the post-war years, Americans threw away or stored in attics their old Orientals and bought the new wall-to-wall carpeting. In Europe, where large numbers of rugs were destroyed during the war, Oriental rugs retained their status with European dealers going to the States to buy up discarded rugs.

Until the mid-twentieth century most collectors were generalists. They bought rugs from all of the rug-weaving areas. Since the 1960s the major trend has been towards tribal and nomadic rugs, with many collectors focusing on specific types, such as Turkish, Caucasian, Turkoman, Afshar, donkeybags or prayer rugs.

Collectors come from all walks of life, and they pursue their interest in many ways. There is no one set of characteristics that sums up the Oriental rug collector. But what collectors do all have in common is that they have to become experts in their field. They have to learn to identify a rug by design, technical features, type of wool, aesthetic qualities and rarity. To be able to identify and evaluate are the two crucial skills.

LEFT An Uzbek soumak (circa 1900) with the characteristic eight-pointed star pattern.

Assessing value

BELOW Konya prayer rug (circa 1850) with a cartouche border inspired by seventeenth century rugs from Transylvania.

ABOVE In all likelihood this Ayvíçik rug woven in 1991 has been chemically washed to soften the colours. Ayvíçik rugs are sold without the DOBAG trademark.

Every collector wants to know how he or she can assess the market value of a rug, but it is simply not possible to give a precise answer. Old and antique Oriental rug prices are item-specific and the price of an individual rug can depend on where it is offered for sale – for instance, at a house sale, at an auction or by a dealer.

The price of a rug may also vary depending on whether market prices are rising or falling; whether the rug is offered for sale in a city which has many collectors or none; whether the city is a large or small one; and whether the collectors are interested in the particular rug type at the time.

Old and antique rugs are best compared to paintings. Prices are variable depending on these same types of factor. The market value of an individual Oriental rug at a given point in time is reliably calculable only on new rugs where there is a known wholesale price.

Collectors who choose to rely on their own knowledge and expertise when buying rugs must attend auctions and subscribe to their catalogues in order to observe price movements. Dealers' quoted prices are another source of information, as is attendance at trade fairs.

Only by keeping in touch with these resources can a collector have a sense of the market. Even then, the estimated price of a given rug by knowledgeable collectors can vary greatly.

Evaluating an antique Oriental rug

There are several general criteria that should be considered when inspecting a rug and deciding whether or not to buy.

Condition The rug's completeness; the condition of the pile, edges and ends; existence of moth damage and stains; and evidence of repair.

Colour Should be well-matched, harmonious and typical of the type; natural or synthetic dyes; and if there is abrash, does it add to or detract from the design?

Rarity Are there many more like it or is it a one-of-a-kind weaving?

Wool quality Is it typical of the type? Assess and categorize the texture and feel to the hand: soft/harsh, oily/dry, lustrous/dull and fragile/durable.

Function Is it a floor rug, bag or festive trapping? Is it a nomadic, village or city weaving?

Age Do the colours, design, condition, patterns, technical features and wool conform to the age cited?

Aesthetic merit Do you like the colour and design?

Price Is this reasonable, given the other factors; how soon will you see another example, is there basis for a 'fair market value'?

LEFT Woven with handspun wool and dyed with natural dyes, the design on this new Turkish kelim dates from the nineteenth century.

Read all about it

Any type of collecting requires dedication, education, time and money. The only way to avoid expending all but the latter is to find a dealer or auction house and rely on their advice. Most collectors, however, choose to do their own searching and buying from a variety of sources. For many collectors 'the pleasure is in the search'.

To educate yourself about Oriental rugs involves reading, visiting dealers and auction houses to see quantities of rugs, meeting other collectors, visiting museums and exhibitions, and attending conferences and trade fairs.

Rug literature comes in several forms and it includes exhibition catalogues and books by experts. In spite of the large number of publications, many quickly go out of print and are therefore hard to find. For specialized literature you need to go to a library or contact a specialist supplier. Most of the latter do their business by catalogue sales or mail order. Some who deal internationally are:

ABOVE Exhibiting five different flatweave techniques, the crosses on this Baluchi saltbag (circa 1920) are silk.

Myrna Bloom – East/West Room, 3139 Alpin Drive, Dresher, PA 19025 USA.

Dennis Marquand, PO Box 1187, Culver City, CA 90232 USA.

The Rug Book Shop, 2603 Talbot Road, Baltimore, MD 21216 USA.

International General, PO Box 305, New York, NY 10013 USA.

Abington Books, Little Abington, Cambridge CBI 6BQ UK.

Uta Hulsey, Postfach 34, D–4230 Wesel, Germany.

Only two periodicals are published for collectors of Oriental rugs. Both are bi-monthly and are sold primarily by subscription. Since they differ considerably in content, most collectors subscribe to both.

Oriental Rug Review, PO Box 709, Meredith, NH 03253, USA.

Hali Magazine, Kingsgate House, Kingsgate Place, London NW6 4TA, UK.

RIGHT Yomud torba (circa 1890). A torba is a long shallow bag.

Dealers

Many collectors find a dealer with whom they have a good rapport and who they trust. The dealer gets to know what types of rug interest them and when such rugs come along, they will bring them to the collector's attention. The dealer/collector relationship is one that needs to be carefully cultivated by both parties. Dealers want to sell; collectors want to acquire.

Rug societies

Another way of learning is from other collectors. Most collectors like to compare pieces, share knowledge and most importantly, compare prices. This is done through Oriental rug societies. You will find information about the societies in the periodicals listed on page 58, and by contacting museum curatorial staff and auction house specialists.

Museums

Museums with noteworthy collections include the following:

Victoria and Albert Museum, London, UK; Metropolitan Museum of Art, New York, USA;
Textile Museum, Washington DC, USA; Museum of Art, Philadelphia, PA, USA; City Art Museum, St Louis, MO, USA; Museum of Fine Arts, San Francisco, CA, USA; Museum of Islamic Art, Berlin, Germany; Museum für Angewandte Kunst, Vienna, Austria;
Iparmuveszeti Museum, Budapest, Hungary;
Gulbenkian Museum, Lisbon, Portugal;
Turk ve Islam Eserleri Museum, Istanbul, Turkey.

Conferences

The major conferences are sponsored by the Textile Museum, Washington, DC (annually), the American Conference on Oriental Rugs (biennially) and the International Conference on Oriental Carpets (triennially in the UK, Europe and the USA in rotation). These conferences normally last from one to three days.

LEFT This Bijar rug (circa 1900) shows the hallmarks village weaving: the hardshang pattern is angular due to imprecise drawing, and the corners illustrate failed attempts at reconciling.

Where to buy

BELOW A Kuba rug (circa 1880) has an interlocking main border pattern that is closely associated with Caucasian rugs.

The most important decision you'll make as a collector is buying your first rug. Not until you have one in your home can it be studied, felt by hand and foot and integrated to determine how captivated you will be by Oriental rugs. Only in this way can you begin to sense what rug collecting is all about. In the long run, the first purchase will either be loved for sentimental reasons or hated. It may be kept as a reminder of mistakes to be avoided or the first rug you sell. Once the first purchase is made, decisions about what and where to buy in the future can be made. That decision will depend largely on your personality, time, special interests, where you live and your budget.

Dealers are one of the major sources of antique Oriental rugs. Although there has been a resurgence of interest in rug collecting in the past twenty-five years, there has not been a corresponding increase in the number of dealers. The vast majority of dealers sell new rugs; only a few specialize in old and antique ones, and most are in large cities.

Auctions are another important source, not only for buying but also for seeing many rugs at one time. Many of the major auction houses in most countries hold specialized sales of Oriental rugs. Usually the rugs may be viewed for one or more days beforehand.

Viewing is a good way to familiarize yourself with a wide variety of rugs. A dealer rarely has an inventory equal to that of a major sale. During this time you can inspect the rugs for condition and wear. Advice on what a rug may sell for is available from the house specialist. But you can never be sure what a rug will fetch until the auctioneer says 'Sold'.

CHAPTER EIGHT

GLOSSARY OF ORIENTAL RUGS

BELOW A Luri kelim (circa 1800) showing many of the features of nomadic rugs: abrash, limited colour range, irregular edges and various coloured warps.

Abrash Variations of density in a colour seen in a carpet by irregular horizontal washes; caused by the wool being dyed at different times in different batches of a colour, which is of unequal density.

Alum Double sulphate of aluminium and potassium used as a mordant.

Aniline Chemical dye, a derivative of coal-tar. First produced in the 1860s and ubiquitous in the Middle East from the 1880s. Most frequently encountered in the red-blue-purple range. Colours are very fugitive; a bright orange-pink will fade at the tip to walnut-brown.

Boteh Widespread pattern of Persian origin. Resembles a pear or pine cone. Best known in Europe as the principal motif of the Paisley pattern.

Ch'ang Chinese endless knot. As the inextricable knot of destiny, the seventh of the Eight Buddhist Symbols.

Chinese fret Interlocking swastika pattern. Often called wan. Wan is the character for 10,000 – a swastika.

Chrome dye A fast synthetic dye mordanted with potassium bichromate. This, and other more recent synthetic colours, are now used in all the major rug weaving areas of the world. Although fast, the colours are harsh and dead.

Cochineal Scarlet red similar to but more brilliant than lac. Obtained from the crushed bodies of an insect native to Mexico and the West Indies, and imported into Europe from the sixteenth century and into the Middle East at the end of the eighteenth century.

Compound-weave Technical term for pieces made with more than one set of either warp or weft elements, or both. Form of flatweaving.

Damascene After Damascus. Process of decorating steel by etching, inlaying gold or silver, or encrusting, so as to produce watered effect. In old carpet literature used to describe either Mamluk carpets or certain designs found on Anatolian pieces. Describes a design effect, and some scholars supposed that the carpets had originated in Damascus.

Djidjim Refers to either a wall hanging/entrance hanging, or to a weaving technique in which flat-woven strips are joined together to form the completed piece.

Ends The outer edges of the rug on the short axis often woven in the kelim technique (pile-woven ends or skirts are frequently found on Turkoman pieces); the fringes found on carpets are the free ends of the warp threads.

Escutcheon Shield-shaped medallion often found on Persian carpets as appendages on either side of a large central medallion on the long axis.

Gol Henai Floral pattern associated with Persian rugs and said to be based on the Henna shrub or the garden balsam. Found on carpets from Hamadan and environs, and in schematic form on Kashgai weavings.

Hejira or Hijra The beginning of the Muhammedan calendar, 16 July, AD 622. Rugs dated with a year of the Hejira can be converted to the Christian equivalent by: dividing the Hejira year by 33.7, subtracting the result from the original date and then adding 622.

Herati Also called the mahi or fish pattern. As its name implies this floral pattern is supposed to have originated in east Persia. Consists of a repeat of a flower head bracketed by two serrate-edged lanceolate leaves. Probably the most used of all Oriental floral designs.

Indigo Blue dye obtained from the leaves of the indigo plant. Native to India, from whence most of the leaves used in the preparation of the dye in Persia were exported. The dye was prepared from a fermented compound of crushed indigo leaves, red clay slip, potash, grape sugar and slaked lime.

Jufti 'False' knot, either Turkish or Persian, whereby the knots are tied to four, not two, warp threads, thus coarsening the weave and halving the time involved in production. Became prevalent in Persia in the late nineteenth century, although for a time it was banned.

Kelim Also spelled kilim, khilim, kileem, gilim, ghilim, gelim, dilim, etc. Form of flat-weaving associated principally with Anatolia.

RIGHT Woven in 1992, this Gabbeh rug is woven with natural dyes and handspun wool. The design is based on a traditional abstract pictorial.

Kermes Crushed female body of an insect that gives a red similar to cochineal and lac. The insect breeds on the Kermes oak. Its use in carpets has never been satisfactorily established.

Kufic Form of Arabic script; its visual format is used as a decorative motif in the borders of Oriental carpets, especially those from Anatolia. Named after an erroneous ascription to Kufa(h) in Mesopotamia. The principal script of the Koran. Other Arabic or Persian scripts include al-ma'il, nashki and its variant nastaliq, ta'liq, rihani, thuluth and shikasta.

Lac or laq Name given to a brilliant deep purple-red obtained from melting and straining the resinous excretions of the *Tachardia lacca*, a scale insect native to India which covers the twigs of certain trees in a resinous substance for the purpose of immuring the female of the species. The red dye, like that of cochineal and kermes, is the extract of the female bodies of the insect, which in this case are gathered with the resin.

Lampas Weaving so that the pattern is raised in relief against the ground. A form of embroidery.

Madder Deep red-brown dye.

Mina Khani Floral pattern said to have been named after Mina Khan, although this is certainly apocryphal. Repeat pattern of large palmettes and small white flowers contained in a lattice of stems. Stylized geometrical versions found in certain tribal carpets, such as those of the Baluchi.

Mordant Chemical substance with which the wool is treated in order to fix the dye colour. Can itself affect the eventual colour and can be corrosive.

Palas Caucasian name for kelim.

Palmette A flower head of heart-shape with many radiating lobes or petals.

Pomegranate rind Gives a dull yellow dye.

Quatrefoil Medallion with four rounded lobe sections.

Saph Prayer rug with multiple mihrabs.

Sarkdy or Sharkyoy Name for kelims made in Thrace.

Selvedge The outer warps of the rug on the long sides, which are overcast to form firm, braided edges. On many tribal pieces, further strengthened with goat's hair.

Shah Abbas Floral design of large palmettes. Found on two- and three-plane lattice vase carpets.

Sileh Possibly a corruption of a Caucasian place name. A form of Soumak, sileh usually refers to pieces woven with rows of large S-motifs thought to represent the dragon motif degenerated to virtual abstraction.

Soumak Also Sumak, Summak, Sumacq, Sumakh. Thought to be a corruption of Shemaka, town in south-east Caucasus. Technique of progressive weft wrapping.

Spandrels Architectural term for the space between the curve of an arch and the enclosing mouldings. Thus the space immediately above the arch of the mihrab in a prayer rug.

Swastika A hooked cross. Chinese symbol for 10,000 (wan) and happiness. In many cultures, a symbol of the sun. An extraordinarily ubiquitous symbol, found contemporaneously as far apart as Pre-Columbian America and China, which appears in the work of almost all known cultures.

Tiraz Weaving factory set up under Royal patronage.

Tchintamani Chinese Buddhist symbol thought by some scholars to be the origin of the balls-and-stripe motif found on Ushak carpets and other Turkish weavings and textiles.

RIGHT Sarouk carpet (circa 1890) with lobed medallion and pendants. Note that the corners are unreconciled.

Verneh Thought to be a corruption of a now unknown Caucasian place name. Technically, these pieces are either Soumak or brocaded rugs (or sometimes a mixture of both), while stylistically the name usually applies to pieces woven with a design of squares, containing either geometric motifs, or a mixture of geometric and animal motifs, especially long-tailed birds.

Vine leaves Give a yellow dye (as do autumnal apple leaves).

Waqf The gift from a private individual to a religious institution such as a mosque.

Warp Longitudinal threads forming part of the foundation of a carpet.

Weft Latitudinal threads forming part of the foundation of a carpet.

Weld Extract of the *Reselda lutuola* plant which gives a yellow dye.

Whey Watery part of milk used in combination with madder to give a particular rose-red colour found on certain Sultanabad carpets.

Yin-Yang Chinese symbol of the female-male elements. Two interlocked foetal motifs in a circle.